30-SECOND
NAPOLEON

30-SECOND
NAPOLEON

THE 50 FUNDAMENTALS OF HIS LIFE, STRATEGIES AND LEGACY,
EACH EXPLAINED IN HALF A MINUTE

Editor
Charles J. Esdaile

Contributors
Philip Dwyer
Charles J. Esdaile
Alan Forrest
Michael Leggiere
Alexander Mikaberidze
Frederick C. Schneid

Illustrations
Steve Rawlings

IVY PRESS

This paperback edition published in the UK in 2019 by
Ivy Press
An imprint of The Quarto Group
The Old Brewery, 6 Blundell Street
London N7 9BH, United Kingdom
T (0)20 7700 6700 **F** (0)20 7700 8066
www.QuartoKnows.com

First published in hardback in 2017

© 2017 Quarto Publishing plc

British Library Cataloguing-in-
Publication Data
A catalogue record for this
book is available from the
British Library.

ISBN: 978-1-78240-755-3

This book was conceived,
designed and produced by
Ivy Press
58 West Street, Brighton, BN1 2RA, UK

Publisher **Susan Kelly**
Creative Director **Michael Whitehead**
Editorial Director **Tom Kitch**
Art Director **James Lawrence**
Project Editor **Caroline Earle**
Designer **Ginny Zeal**
Commissioning Editor **Sophie Collins**
Picture Researcher **Katie Greenwood**
Glossaries **Charles J. Esdaile**
Assistant Editor **Jenny Campbell**

Cover image: Shutterstock/Everett – Art

Printed in China

10 9 8 7 6 5 4 3 2

CONTENTS

INTRODUCTION

Charles J. Esdaile

Since his death in 1821 in British captivity on the
remote island of St Helena, the figure of Napoleon Bonaparte remains
the subject of vigorous debate, sometimes even vituperative debate.
On the one side, not counting proud Frenchmen determined to stand
by a national hero in the face of perfidious Albion, are those motivated
by a romantic attachment to ideals of liberty and democracy (ideals
which Napoleon himself frankly despised) or by a still more romantic
attachment to lost causes, together with those who have been seduced
by a propaganda machine that is in many ways as superb today as it was
in the days of the Napoleonic Empire. And, on the same side are those –
let us be quite clear about this – who have followed the advice given
by Napoleon to the little band of courtiers who shared his final exile to
the effect that they would be able to make their fortunes by telling his
story. On the other side are those who rather see the French ruler as little
more than an ambitious warlord (albeit one of considerable brilliance)
bent only on establishing a colonial empire in the heart of Europe. As
the great Dutch historian, Pieter Geyl, showed in his seminal *Napoleon
For and Against*, these two belligerent camps have fought it out on the
same lines for decade after decade in a war that has never ended and is
never likely to end: it is literally as easy to follow the eagles, or, indeed,
fight against them, now as it was in 1815.

This slim work does not pretend to be a contribution to that debate
(or, rather, shouting match: if ever there was a dialogue of the deaf, it is
the Napoleon controversy). Rather it is an attempt to provide a brief
introduction to one of the most recognizable figures in all history, a figure,
moreover, who is one of extraordinary interest even to those who loathe
the man and everything he represents. To look for anything even remotely
approaching the full story in its pages would be ridiculous, but it can yet
be hoped that they will provide a spur to further reading.

In brief, however, for what does Napoleon really stand? Here, it is, alas,
necessary to begin by casting aside romantic notions of a selfless French

patriot, a champion of the French Revolution or even a precursor of the present-day European Union. The reality was very different: Napoleon was little but a soldier of fortune, a conqueror bent on personal aggrandisement who was in the end brought down, not by the concerted hostility of the *ancien régime*, but rather by his own megalomania and lust for glory. That said, warlord though he was, he was a warlord of extraordinary vision and talent, an advocate of reform who stood for

Napoleon at Jena
Napoleon's victory over the Prussian army at Jena and Auerstädt in 1806 cemented his reputation as a brilliant military strategist.

rational and efficient government and such principles as equality before the law and the career open to talents. More than that, almost invariably envisaged in the simple garb represented by his low black hat and plain grey coat, the Emperor is thought of not so much of an emperor, as, if not everyman, then at the very least everyman made good. As such he appears as a veritable dream come true, and it is, perhaps, above all this that makes him so attractive to so many people.

Putting together this book represented a considerable challenge: indeed, at the beginning the task of telling the story of Napoleon's life and times in just 50 short essays seemed insuperable, and not just insuperable but pointless – what on earth could the volume that might eventually result add to the existing literature? To take this last question first, the answer that now comes to mind is 'a surprising amount'. Much has had to be pared to the bone or stripped away altogether, but contained in the pages will be found not just the bare details of the imperial biography, but also an attempt at a critical re-assessment that draws on the latest academic research. As for how it was put together, the seven chapters can be divided into three chapters (**Life**, **Victories** and **Defeats**) that together provide a brief narrative, two chapters (**Marshals** and **Tools**) that discuss some of the men, methods and institutions that played a part in Napoleon's rise to power and subsequent military success, one chapter that looks at the political and social situation from which the French ruler sprang (**Context**) and, finally, one chapter (**Empire**) that looks at the territories of the grand empire and seeks to chart their experience of Napoleonic rule.

Finally a brief guide to using this slim work. Throughout the volume, you will find each subject contained on a single left-hand page, with selected imagery on the right-hand page. The main entry – the 30-Second History – provides the most in-depth treatment of the topic. In the margin at left, the 3-Second Shot encapsulates the topic in a single sentence and, below, the 3-Minute Code elaborates on the theme at slightly greater length. To the right, meanwhile, will generally be one or more 3-Second Biographies which list relevant individuals with significant connections to the theme under discussion, together with some cross references to other entries. Finally, at the end of the book will be found some brief suggestions for those who wish to take their reading further.

MAJOR BATTLES OF THE NAPOLEONIC WARS
Locations of the key battles and sieges – the map shows 1812 country borders

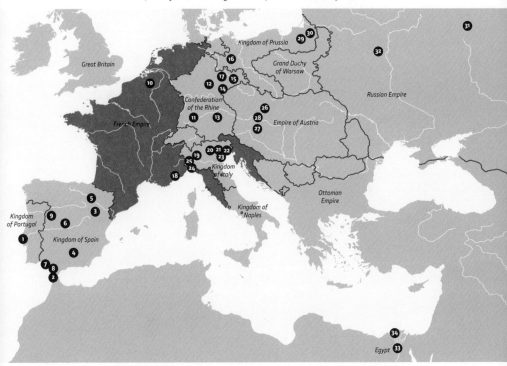

Present-day Portugal

1   1808 Battle of Vimeiro

Present-day Spain

2   1805 Battle of Trafalgar

3   1808 & 1809 Siege of Zaragoza

4   1808 Battle of Bailén

5   1808 Battle of Tudela

6   1809 Battle of Talavera

7   1810–12 Siege of Càdiz

8   1811 Battle of Barrosa

9   1812 Battle of Salamanca

Present-day Belgium

10   1815 Battle of Waterloo

Present-day Germany

11   1805 Battle of Ulm

12   1806 Battle of Jena-Auerstädt

13   1809 Battle of Eckmühl

14   1813 Battle of Lützen

15   1813 Battle of Bautzen

16   1813 Battle of Dennewitz

17   1813 Battle of Leipzig

Present-day Italy

18   1796 Battle of Millesimo

19   1796 Battle of Lodi

20   1796 Battle of Lonato

21   1796 Battle of Castiglione

22   1796 Battle of Arcola

23   1797 Battle of Rivoli

24   1800 Siege of Genoa

25   1800 Battle of Marengo

Present-day Czech Republic

26   1805 Battle of Austerlitz

Present-day Austria

27   1809 Battle of Aspern-Essling

28   1809 Battle of Wagram

Present-day Russia

29   1807 Battle of Eylau

30   1807 Battle of Friedland

31   1812 Battle of Borodino

Present-day Belarus

32   1812 Battle of Berezina

Present-day Egypt

33   1798 Battle of the Pyramids

34   1798 Battle of the Nile

The French Empire

CONTEXTS

ancien régime Also referred to as the 'Old Order', the *ancien régime* is a term used to describe the political and social situation of continental Europe prior to the French Revolution, its chief characteristics being absolute monarchy and the survival of both corporate privilege and various forms of feudalism.

anti-clericalism A term used to describe hostility to the Catholic Church. At the level of the streets exemplified by mockery of the clergy and, on occasion, violence; at the level of rulers and governments, it found expression in attempts to reduce the power of the papacy, to subject the Church to greater state control and to abolish the religious orders.

The Age of Reason The 'Age of Reason' (also 'the Enlightenment') is a term used to describe the period 1650–1789, the reason being that this was a moment when the European cultural élite made a collective discovery to the effect that the workings of the natural world and, indeed, human society, could be understood and investigated through the application of intellect.

Bourbons The French royal family at the time of the French Revolution. Other branches of the family occupied the thrones of Spain and Naples.

The Grand Tour In the eighteenth century the 'Grand Tour' was a central part of the education of any gentleman. Singly or in groups, young men would travel from place to place along more or less fixed routes through France, Germany and Italy, visiting famous monuments, admiring works of art, learning about advances in agriculture and industry and generally acquiring a veneer of courtesy and sophistication.

Panthéon Originally a church built in the Latin quarter in Paris in the period 1757–90, the Panthéon was modelled on the temple of the same name in Rome. No sooner had it been consecrated than it was seized by the regime that had emerged from the French Revolution and transformed into a mausoleum for the remains of national heroes.

Russo-Turkish War (1787–91) Beaten by the Russians in a series of wars in the course of the eighteenth century, in 1787 the Ottoman Empire tried to reverse the advance of Russian rule by demanding the evacuation of the recently occupied Crimea. In response, Russia went to war again, the struggle ending with the loss of yet more Turkish territory.

Seven Years' War (1756–60) A struggle that pitted Britain and Prussia against Austria, France, Russia and Spain, the Seven Years' War devastated large parts of central Europe and also spread to India and North America. The fighting is particularly notable for the series of dramatic victories won by the Prussian monarch, Frederick II.

War of the Austrian Succession (1740–8) This war emerged out of the desire of the Prussians to seize fresh territory from Austria. Using the supposedly illegal accession to the throne of the Archduchess Maria Teresa as a pretext, the Prussians duly invaded Silesia, and quickly gained the support of France and Spain, but Austria was supported by Britain. The fighting at length ended with a compromise peace.

War of the Bavarian Succession (1778–9) Like the struggles of 1700–14 and 1740–8, the War of the Bavarian Succession was motivated by a succession crisis. Fearing that the death of the ruler of Bavaria without issue would lead to the Austrians seizing control, Prussia and Saxony sent troops to ensure that this did not happen. However, there was little fighting, the Austrians electing to back down rather than face yet another major conflict.

War of the Spanish Succession (1700–14) A conflict brought about by the death without issue of the last Habsburg ruler of Spain. Determined to extend his power, King Louis XIV of France sought to place one of his nephews on the throne, only to face furious resistance on the part of Britain and Austria.

CORSICA

the 30-second history

The Corsica into which Napoleon was born on 15 August 1769 was an important formative influence on the future French ruler. Contrary to the impression that the latter was sometimes inclined to project, the Bonapartes were a substantial land-owning family who were both nobles and powerful members of the local urban élite (like the rest of the Corsican gentry, they lived in the towns rather than on their estates). Thus, from his earliest beginnings, Napoleon was instilled with a deep fear and loathing of the populace, the poverty-stricken people of the Corsican mountains being renowned for banditry, cruelty, superstition and ignorance. However, sent to military school in France at an early age, as a provincial who could barely speak French and had a foreign name (he was born not Napoléon Bonaparte, but Nabuleone Buonaparte), Napoleon experienced scorn and derision. To fear of the common people was therefore quickly added burning ambition, which at first expressed itself in a fierce Corsican patriotism: prior to its acquisition by France in 1768, Corsica had been engaged in a prolonged war of independence against the Genoese, and so Napoleon fantasized about leading his homeland to freedom and becoming a second Pasquale Paoli.

3-SECOND SHOT
Forced by the contortions of Corsican politics to flee to France in 1793, Napoleon responded by cutting all links with his native island and becoming more French than the French.

3-MINUTE CODE
Prior to Napoleon's birth, the Corsican élite had been engaged in a long struggle for independence. A full-scale revolt that broke out in 1729 had been defeated by the island's Genoese masters in 1736, but in 1755 revolt broke out again under Pasquale Paoli. Unable to impose their rule, the Genoese handed the island over to France in 1768, and thus it was that Napoleon was born a Frenchman.

RELATED TOPIC
See also
PASQUALE DI PAOLI
page 40

3-SECOND BIOGRAPHY
CARLO BUONAPARTE
1746–85
Napoleon's father, Carlo Buonaparte was initially a strong supporter of Corsican independence but later turned collaborator

30-SECOND TEXT
Charles J. Esdaile

Mountainous and poverty-stricken, Corsica had a long history of producing adventurers and soldiers of fortune.

ENLIGHTENED ABSOLUTISM

the 30-second history

RELATED TOPICS
See also
THE ENLIGHTENMENT
page 18

FRENCH REVOLUTION
page 22

NEO-CLASSICISM
page 28

3-SECOND SHOT
Enlightened absolutism is a term used to describe the monarchical reformism common in eighteenth-century Europe that constituted one of the chief influences underpinning Napoleon's domestic policies.

3-MINUTE CODE
The enlightened absolutists represent an extraordinary gallery of talent. Catherine II of Russia, Charles III of Spain, Frederick II of Prussia and their fellows were towering figures who assembled teams of great vision and ability. To regard the *ancien régime* as static, let alone antiquated, would therefore be very wrong. What is the case, however, is that they faced formidable domestic enemies who were often able to frustrate their best efforts.

At its weakest in France (hence, in part, the Revolution of 1789 and, with it, the rise of Napoleon), enlightened absolutism is the name given to a style of monarchy that was once portrayed in terms of paternalism and benevolence, the idea being that the monarchs of Europe were dedicated to the welfare of their subjects. This, however, can no longer be viewed as a satisfactory explanation. While it is true that prosperity was a common goal and even that some monarchs engaged in social reform, the intention was essentially to increase the revenues of the state and ensure domestic stability. Thus, what motivated monarchs was power and prestige: locked in constant rivalry with their fellow rulers, they needed strong armed forces and therefore strong states too, and this implied a drive towards centralization, economic development and greater administrative efficiency. Yet this was not incompatible with an interest in the Enlightenment. Hence the anti-clericalism that was also a common characteristic of the movement: along with the nobility everywhere, in Catholic parts of Europe the Church stood squarely in the way of enlightened absolutism, and most states therefore saw at least some attempt to clip its wings.

3-SECOND BIOGRAPHIES
MARQUES DE POMBAL
1699–1782
The central figure of enlightened absolutism in Portugal, Pombal introduced a series of measures designed to boost Portuguese commerce and curb the authority of the Catholic Church

CONDE DE FLORIDABLANCA
1728–1808
Chief minister of Spain from 1778 to 1792, Floridablanca was typical of the reformist officials who formed the backbone of enlightened absolutism, and is remembered for his reforms in the area of administration

30-SECOND TEXT
Charles J. Esdaile

The enlightened absolutists presided over an age of great cultural advance.

THE ENLIGHTENMENT

the 30-second history

The Enlightenment was the great intellectual movement that dominated the eighteenth century. Across Europe, this saw men of letters throw themselves into wide-ranging discussions of society, while at the same time exploring such areas as history, geography and the natural sciences. Central to everything was the belief that with the aid of reason mankind could come to understand the mysteries of the natural, physical and human worlds and apply that knowledge to the pursuit of progress: hence the alternative name of the Age of Reason. Literary, cultural and scientific life flourished and the period saw the establishment of numerous learned societies. Many of the leading figures of the movement were French – D'Alembert, Voltaire, Diderot and Lavoisier – but others include the Swiss Rousseau; the Spaniard Jovellanos; the German Kant; and the Britons Gibbon, Hume and Smith. Eager to pursue economic development and a growth in the power of the state, many rulers of Europe patronized and encouraged these thinkers, and some have argued that in doing so they helped sign the death warrant of the *ancien régime*. Coming to power in the wake of the French Revolution, meanwhile, Napoleon drew heavily on the principles of the Enlightenment in his domestic policy.

RELATED TOPICS
See also
ENLIGHTENED ABSOLUTISM
page 16

FRENCH REVOLUTION
page 22

NEO-CLASSICISM
page 28

3-SECOND BIOGRAPHIES
FRANÇOIS-MARIE AROUET
1694–1778
Universally referred to by his pen name of Voltaire, Arouet was one of the most prodigious and influential writers of his day

EDWARD GIBBON
1737–94
Author of the widely read *Decline and Fall of the Roman Empire* Gibbon attributed the collapse of Rome to the abandonment of republican virtues and the rise of Christianity

30-SECOND TEXT
Charles J. Esdaile

In a trend Napoleon was keen to continue, the Enlightenment gave birth to modern scholarship.

28 June 1712
Born in Geneva; mother dies eight days later of childbirth fever

1722
Fostered to Calvinist minister

1725
Apprenticed to an engraver; three years later flees Geneva and migrates to Turin

1732
First comes into contact with the world of letters

1739
Migrates to Lyons and is employed as a tutor

1742
Moves to Paris; a year later is employed as secretary to French ambassador to Venice

1745
Settles down with Thérèse Levasseur with whom he has five children but insists that they are all abandoned to Paris' foundling hospital

1749–50
Contributes to Diderot's *Encyclopedia*

1752
Wins notoriety by turning down the substantial royal pension offered him for his opera, *The Village Soothsayer* (though not a musician, Rousseau loved music and had experimented with a new form of musical notation)

1754
Returns to Geneva

1755
Publishes *The Discourse on Inequality*

1761
Publishes *Julie or the New Héloïse*

1762
Publishes *The Social Contract*; flees Geneva a second time

1765–70
Writes *The Confessions* (published 1782)

1772
Publishes *Considerations on the Government of Poland* and *Constitutional Project for Corsica*

1772–6
Writes *Dialogues*; *Rousseau, Judge of Jean-Jacques* (published 1782)

2 July 1778
Dies of apoplectic stroke

1794
Declared a national hero by the Convention; Rousseau's body reburied in the Panthéon

JEAN-JACQUES ROUSSEAU

The son of a Geneva watchmaker, Jean-Jacques Rousseau grew up in a district full of artisans angry at the hold which the local élite had on the city government, the result being that from an early age he was surrounded by political discussion of a radical nature. Apprenticed to an engraver, he ran away rather than face his repeated beatings and was taken in by a group of Catholics out to bring as many Protestants as possible to the true faith. Under their influence, Rousseau duly converted, and for the next few years he worked in a series of tutoring posts in northern Italy. Eventually moving to Paris, he was drawn into the world of the Enlightenment thinkers known as the *philosophes*, and was soon publishing political pamphlets, of which one, the *Discourse on the Arts and Sciences* won a major prize. Returning to Geneva (where he perforce reconverted to Protestantism), he embarked on the life of an author in earnest.

There followed a string of major works in which three were treatises of political philosophy – the *Discourse on Inequality* (1755) and *Of the Social Contract* and *Emile or On Education* (both 1762) – and *Julie or the New Héloise* (1761), a romantic novel. All these works challenging established orthodoxy in one way or another, Rousseau was forced to flee Geneva and thereupon spent many years in exile, in the process falling out with many leading figures of the Enlightenment. Conscious, perhaps, of the personal failings that had caused these disputes, between 1765 and 1770 he wrote a long autobiography known as *The Confessions*. Two last political tracts followed in the form of draft constitutions for Poland (a state then in the grip of much turmoil) and Corsica, but his health began to fail and in 1778 he had a severe stroke and died.

Rousseau's influence was immense. A difficult and in many ways somewhat unpleasant character, he yet believed that, in its historic state of nature, mankind was perfect, and that, if it was now corrupt, this was because it had been corrupted by the workings of society. Though Rousseau never in fact said as much, the inference was that society must be rebuilt so as to restore the natural order, the result being that his works became the veritable bible of the French Revolution. Napoleon himself asserted: 'Had there been no Rousseau, there would have been no Revolution.'

Charles J. Esdaile

FRENCH REVOLUTION

the 30-second history

3-SECOND SHOT
Influenced by
Enlightenment ideals, the
French Revolution shook
France and the rest of the
world, and produced the
rise of a Napoleon deeply
shocked by the violence
of the crowd.

3-MINUTE CODE
On his return from Egypt in
1789, Napoleon discovered
a Republican movement
divided between those who
believed in a conservative
regime based on the
interests of property and
those who wanted to
secure the support of the
people by pushing radical
social reform. Invited to
help the former by political
thinker, Emmanuel Sièyes,
Napoleon duly organized
the coup that brought him
to power as, in the first
instance, First Consul.

The episode at the heart of Napoleon's early career, the Revolution that broke out in France in 1789 was a complex situation. Certainly not the bourgeois affair of Marxist legend, rather it was the fruit of two movements that were in many ways opposed to one another. On the one hand, powerful elements of the élite were convinced that the French state was in desperate need of reform, and, on the other, the populace was assailed by periodic subsistence crises and often burdened by heavy feudal dues. In 1789 circumstances conspired to link these two issues together; the result was a great explosion that destroyed the *ancien régime* and turned France into a constitutional monarchy. This, however, was not the end of the story: with public opinion split between those who wished to keep change within certain bounds and those who wanted to push it on still further, politics descended into a bitter fratricidal struggle. While 1792 saw France transformed into a radical Republic, in 1794 the Right hit back and established a more conservative regime, only for this to collapse in turn and thereby make way for Napoleon's rise to power in 1799.

RELATED TOPICS
See also
THE ENLIGHTENMENT
page 18

JEAN-JACQUES ROUSSEAU
page 20

3-SECOND BIOGRAPHIES
EMMANUEL SIEYÈS
1748–1836
Though a Catholic priest,
in 1789 Sieyès wrote the
immensely influential 'What
is the Third Estate?', while
it was he who called in
Napoleon in 1799

MAXIMILIEN DE ROBESPIERR
1758–94
A ruthless pragmatist who
believed that the survival of
the Revolution was dependen
on an alliance with the people
Robespierre introduced price
controls and a democratic
constitution, only to be
overthrown, arrested and
subsequently guillotined

30-SECOND TEXT
Charles J. Esdaile

*Born in hope, the
French Revolution
led to a turmoil that
Napoleon hated and
sought to end.*

THE INDUSTRIAL REVOLUTION

the 30-second history

RELATED TOPIC
See also
WATERLOO
page 108

An extraordinary transformative process that built the world we know today, the Industrial Revolution was born in Britain in the mid-eighteenth century on the back of prodigious wealth flowing in from, first, the slave trade; second, the profits generated by Britain's West Indian colonies; and, third, the demand for cotton cloth and other products that resulted from colonial growth. So great was this demand that it could only be satisfied by mass production, and there therefore emerged the new notion of the factory, an establishment in which goods could be produced cheaply and efficiently with the aid of machinery. At first, the motive power was water, but from the 1770s onwards the discovery of how to harness steam produced a further step-change in the rate of development. With the factory, meanwhile, came rapid urbanization: forced to work very long hours, workers needed to live close to their places of work. Also seen were serious social problems: workers endured terrible conditions, while many traditional trades were undercut by factory production and the artisans concerned rapidly proletarianized. In France, meanwhile, Napoleon was an enthusiastic proponent of industrialization, lending much support to both iron and cotton, while at the same time taking a very hard line against trade-unionism.

3-SECOND SHOT
Though still taking shape at the time of Napoleon, the Industrial Revolution was an important part of the context: Waterloo was won not on Eton's playing fields but in Lancashire's cotton mills.

3-MINUTE CODE
It is often argued that the Industrial Revolution made war between London and Paris inevitable: in brief, Britain needed to crush French growth just as France needed to overthrow British dominance. However, while economic interests were undoubtedly a factor, Britain was also motivated by traditional strategic requirements such as the need to maintain the balance of power in Europe.

3-SECOND BIOGRAPHIES
JAMES WATT
1736–1819
Scottish engineer, Watt greatly improved the power of steam engines through his development of the condenser

RICHARD CRAWSHAY
1739–1810
Proprietor of the great Cyfarthfa ironworks at Merthyr Tydfil, Crawshay ran away from home to make his fortune at the age of 12

ANTOINE LAVOISIER
1743–94
French scientist who contributed to industrial advances through his isolation of such elements as oxygen, hydrogen and sulphur, Lavoisier was guillotined in 1794

30-SECOND TEXT
Charles J. Esdaile

Slower to take off in France, the Industrial Revolution made Britain the 'workshop of the world'.

INTERNATIONAL RELATIONS

the 30-second history

RELATED TOPIC
See also
ENLIGHTENED ABSOLUTISM
page 16

3-SECOND SHOT
The French Revolution did not transform international relations; it merely complicated them through the re-insertion of a France temporarily cowed by the Seven Years' War.

3-MINUTE CODE
Neither the French Revolution or Napoleon ever faced a coalition of states bent on restoring the Bourbon monarchy and turning the clock back to 1789, claims that Europe was plunged into an ideological war being completely untrue. Instead, the powers of Europe to a very large extent remained driven by pre-existing foreign-policy objectives, and for the most part only went to war with France when they felt they absolutely had to. In short, peace was never unattainable.

Napoleon was born into a Europe

gripped by warfare: between 1700 and 1789 there was only one year when the whole continent was at peace. In brief, the powers of Europe were engaged in a constant round of struggles with one another that seemed to have no end. As soon as one gained some territory, another would seek 'compensation' somewhere else, and so there was a chain reaction that continued *ad inifinitum*. To add to the mayhem, all states sought security in offensive and defensive alliances, but this merely increased the insecurity as there was no way of limiting quarrels to just two belligerents: instead, Europe was repeatedly convulsed by massive wars that raged from one end of the continent to the other and involved large coalitions, good examples being the War of the Spanish Succession (1700–14), the War of the Austrian Succession (1740–8), the Seven Years' War (1756–60), the War of the Bavarian Succession (1778–9) and, finally, the Russo-Turkish War (1787–91), which, despite its name, also involved Austria, Sweden and Denmark. With the situation ever more unstable thanks to Prussian and Russian designs on Poland, it is therefore probable that the last decades of the eighteenth century would have seen a major conflict even without the events of the French Revolution.

3-SECOND BIOGRAPHIES
WILLIAM PITT
1759–1806
Prime Minister of Britain from 1783 to 1801 and then again from 1804 to 1806, Pitt appears to fit the stereotype of an *ancien-régime* statesman determined to overthrow the French Revolution at all costs, yet in 1797 he gave serious thought to a compromise peace with France

CLEMENS VON METTERNICH
1773–1859
A Rhenish diplomat who became Austrian Foreign Minister in 1809, Metternich wanted to keep Napoleon in power to ensure that France remained a check on the ambitions of Russia and Prussia

30-SECOND TEXT
Charles J. Esdaile

In the cut-throat world of international relations, Napoleon was at first to reign supreme.

NEO-CLASSICISM

the 30-second history

Neo-Classicism is the name given

to a cultural movement that was very prominent in the second half of the eighteenth century and, especially, the France of the Revolution and Napoleon. Brought about by the popularity of the so-called 'Grand Tour' and the rediscovery of such ancient-world marvels as Pompeii and Paestum, its strongest legacy was in architecture: the Panthéon in Paris is an early example, St George's Hall in Liverpool a very late one. The interest of architects in Roman and Greek models is understandable – their clean lines and simplicity were a complete contrast to the complexity of the hitherto-dominant Baroque and Rococo styles – yet neo-classicism was also very marked throughout the arts, painters, sculptors, writers and poets all drawing much inspiration from the Classical world. Not surprisingly, Napoleon was an ardent follower of the genre, using the respectability that it represented to emphasize the legitimacy of his rule: hence the Consulate, the legion of honour, the eagles carried by his armies, the laurel wreath he used as a crown and, finally, the two triumphal arches built in Paris.

3-SECOND SHOT
Neo-Classicism was an art style that emerged in eighteenth-century France modelled on ancient Rome and chimed precisely with the dreams of grandeur of the young Napoleon.

3-MINUTE CODE
Though primarily associated with the late eighteenth and early nineteenth centuries, Neo-Classicism was also seen throughout the age of imperialism: Victorian Britain provides many examples. It was also much admired by Italian dictator Benito Mussolini, who saw the construction of grandiose buildings such as Milan's railway station as a means of associating his regime with the glories of the Roman Empire.

RELATED TOPICS
See also
THE ENLIGHTENMENT
page 18

ART
page 136

JACQUES-LOUIS DAVID
page 138

3-SECOND BIOGRAPHIES
ANTONIO CANOVA
1757–1822
Italian Neo-Classical sculptor regarded as the greatest artist of his day, Canova produced a nude statue of Napoleon as 'Mars, the Peacemaker' (1806)

PIERRE FONTAINE
1762–1853
French Neo-Classical architect, who, with Charles Percier, was responsible for the Arc de Triomphe du Carrousel

30-SECOND TEXT
Charles J. Esdaile

Fascination with the glories of ancient Rome rendered the late eighteenth century a perfect moment for would-be caesars like Napoleon.

on Latera

LIFE ◑

ancien régime Also referred to as the
'Old Order', the *ancien régime* is a term
used to describe the political and social
situation of continental Europe prior to the
French Revolution, its chief characteristics
being absolute monarchy and the survival
of both corporate privilege and various
forms of feudalism.

Cisalpine Republic Centred on the Po
valley with its capital at Milan, the Cisalpine
Republic was one of a series of satellite
states created by the victorious French
armies in the period 1795–8. Its flag
survived to provide the basis of the
present-day Italian tricolour.

Coup of 18 Brumaire A date in the new
calendar adopted by the newly formed
French Republic in 1792 that corresponds
to 9 November, 18 Brumaire was the day
in 1799 when a Napoleon freshly returned
from Egypt seized power in Paris with
the help of the army.

Ecole Militaire Military academy opened
in Paris in 1760 that to this day remains
France's chief centre for the basic training
of army officers. At the time at which it was
attended by Napoleon, it was known as the
Ecole des Cadets-Gentilhommes – the School
of Gentlemen-Cadets.

émigrés The word *émigré* means 'emigrant',
and in the context of the French Revolution
refers to the thousands of nobles who fled
abroad rather than live under the new regime.

Holy Roman Empire Dating from the middle
of the tenth century, the Holy Roman Empire
was a collection of hundreds of German
principalities, bishoprics and free cities owing
allegiance to a single overlord (from the
sixteenth century onwards the head of the
house of Habsburg). In 1806 it was abolished
whereupon the current emperor, Francis II,
took the title Francis I of Austria.

Republic of Genoa Originally a medieval city
state, Genoa could trace its independence
back to the year 1005. However, in 1796 it
was over-run by Napoleon's forces and
transformed into a satellite state known
as the Ligurian Republic.

Treaty of Campo Formio Signed between Napoleon and his Austrian opponents in October 1797, the Treaty of Campo Formio saw Austria surrender the Duchy of Lombardy in exchange for the territories that the now-defunct Republic of Venice had possessed in northeastern Italy (as well as Lombardy, Napoleon also got Venice's various Aegean islands and territories on the coast of Dalmatia).

Tricolour The red, white and blue flag of the French Republic. Several other three-colour examples date from this period namely the red, white and mid-blue of Holland, the red, white and green of Italy and the red, yellow and black of Belgium.

CHILDHOOD

the 30-second history

3-SECOND SHOT
Napoleon was seemingly a turbulent youth obsessed with competition with his siblings and the idea of personal advancement.

3-MINUTE CODE
Like many (educated) young men of his time, Nabuleone was imbued with the values of the Enlightenment and enthused by the idea of reform. Initially a Corsican nationalist, the defeat of his schemes to rise to the fore in his native island in the wake of the Revolution led him to flee to France and seek his fortune under the tricolour.

Nabuleone, as he was originally called, the second (surviving) child of Carlo Buonaparte, and Letizia Ramolino, was born in Ajaccio, Corsica on 5 August 1769. He spent the first nine years of his life on the island speaking the local Corsican dialect. Nabuleone's childhood hero was Pasquale Paoli, leader of the Corsican independence movement. Nabuleone's father, Carlo, was aligned with the movement to secure Corsica's independence from the Republic of Genoa, but, when this was crushed by the French, rather than flee the island, Carlo turned collaborator. Largely as a result of his connections with the occupying forces Carlo was able to gain scholarships to continue the education of his sons, Joseph and Napoleon. Napoleon was sent to the military academy at Brienne in the north of France in 1778, where he spent the next five years. From Brienne, he was able to gain entry to the prestigious École Militaire in Paris, where he continued his education as an officer. In 1786, after only a year of study, he was commissioned as a second-lieutenant in the artillery, having been away from Corsica for eight years. The previous year his father had died of stomach cancer at the age of 38, thereby leaving the Bonaparte family in the hands of Napoleon, the latter quickly supplanting his more easy-going elder brother, Joseph, as its natural head.

RELATED TOPICS
See also
CORSICA
page 14

PASQUALE DI PAOLI
page 40

3-SECOND BIOGRAPHY
LOUIS DE MARBEUF
1712–86
A senior French commander, Marbeuf was made governor of Corsica when the island was ceded to France by Genoa in 1768. Inveigled by Napoleon's father, Carlo, he quickly became a patron of the Bonaparte family, this later giving rise to rumours that he had a long affair with Letizia Bonaparte

30-SECOND TEXT
Philip Dwyer

Napoleon's childhood and school days are lost in legend, but there is little doubt that from an early age he struck observers as someone of great character and intellect.

JOSEPHINE

the 30-second history

Born Marie-Josèphe Rose Tascher

de La Pagerie in Martinique in 1763, the Empress Josephine (a name given her by Napoleon) married a nobleman named Alexandre de Beauharnais at the age of 16 and had two children by him – Hortense and Eugène. Imprisoned in the Terror, she lost her husband to the guillotine and only just managed to escape execution herself. Released in 1794, Josephine turned her natural wit and beauty to good advantage, and became a woman of some note: for a while, indeed, she was the mistress of Paul de Barras, then the most prominent politician in France. Coming across her in the autumn of 1795, Napoleon immediately fell under her spell, and married her the following March without consulting with his family (absolutely furious at this slight, they would never forgive or accept her). A few days after the marriage, Napoleon left to fight in Italy, whereupon she immediately had an affair. Deeply hurt, Napoleon forgave her, but he probably never trusted or loved her as deeply again and responded with a series of affairs of his own, eventually divorcing her in 1809 when it became obvious that she was not going to fall pregnant to him. Josephine died five years after the divorce.

RELATED TOPIC
See also
MARIE-LOUISE
page 44

3-SECOND SHOT
The relationship between Napoleon and Josephine has gone down in history as one of the great love affairs, but was in fact rather one-sided: while Napoleon loved Josephine passionately, she was indifferent.

3-MINUTE CODE
It is difficult to see what a man of Napoleon's intelligence saw in a woman like Josephine, who may have been charming, but was also calculating, flighty, profligate and vain. She spent far more on clothing and jewels than Marie-Antoinette ever did, but for all that was always extremely popular with the French army and to the very end remained on good terms with her ex-husband.

3-SECOND BIOGRAPHIES
PAUL DE BARRAS
1755–1829
Barras was an unprincipled intriguer of immense corruption who played a leading role in the fall of Robespierre and subsequently secured one of the five seats in the Directory

EUGÈNE DE BEAUHARNAIS
1781–1824
Josephine's son by her first marriage, Eugène married a German princess and served Napoleon as Viceroy of the Kingdom of Italy

HORTENSE DE BEAUHARNAIS
1783–1837
Josephine's daughter by her first marriage. She married Napoleon's younger brother, Louis, only for the match to end in separation

30-SECOND TEXT
Philip Dwyer

Possessed of many faults, Josephine was nonetheless one of the most charismatic women of the age.

ELEVATION

the 30-second history

3-SECOND SHOT
Spurred on by good
fortune, military victory
and his own extraordinary
talent, Napoleon's rise to
power was remarkably
rapid even by the standards
of the Revolution.

3-MINUTE CODE
Being a general was
risky business during
the Revolution: dozens
of generals were killed in
battle, murdered by their
own men or executed
for failing to perform
according to the
requirements of their
political masters. Yet,
thanks to a combination
of good fortune, personal
astuteness and an
undoubted ability to win
battles and enthuse his
troops, Napoleon escaped
unscathed, and, more
than that, navigated his
way to safety.

Two days after his marriage to
Josephine, Napoleon left Paris to take command
of the Army of Italy. Over the next nine months,
he drove the Austrians from Italy, eventually
securing a victorious peace by means of the
Treaty of Campo Formio. During the Italian
campaign, having learned that propaganda
was just as important as military victories, he
founded two newspapers to promote his image
and thereby gained much influence in Paris,
while his ambition was greatly boosted by his
formation of the Cisalpine Republic. With little
to do back in France, Napoleon embraced the
idea of an invasion of Egypt. Landing near
Alexandria, he had soon captured Cairo and
began to harbour wild dreams of marching on
India, even of becoming a new Alexander the
Great. A failed invasion of Palestine soon put
an end to these ambitions, but not even the
destruction of his invasion fleet by Horatio
Nelson at the Battle of the Nile sufficed to
dim his star in France, let alone moderate his
own self-esteem. Abandoning his army to its
fate, he therefore sailed for France and was
very soon plotting to seize control of the
government, a goal which he attained
through the *coup d'état* of 18 Brumaire.

RELATED TOPICS
See also
ITALIAN CAMPAIGN
page 74

MARENGO
page 76

EGYPT
page 94

3-SECOND BIOGRAPHIES
LUCIEN BONAPARTE
1775–1840
The third of the five Bonaparte
brothers, Lucien entered
politics in the wake of the
French Revolution, and in
1799 played a key role in the
Coup of 18 Brumaire

HORATIO NELSON
1758–1805
Perhaps Britain's greatest
naval commander, Nelson
won great victories at the
Nile and Trafalgar

30-SECOND TEXT
Philip Dwyer

By the age of 30,
Napoleon had risen
from obscurity to
become First Consul.
Four years later he
was Emperor.

CAMPAGNES LE CONSEIL DES ANCIENS, adoptant les motifs de la décla-
ration d'urgence, qui précède la résolution ci-après, approuve
DES FRANÇAIS EN IT. l'urgence.

SOUS LES ORDRES

DE BONAPART.

JUSQU'AU

TRAITÉ DE CAMPO-FO...

SECONDE EDITION

Du 19 Brumaire, an 8 de la République

République

Liberté

6922

Le Ministre de la Guerre

COUP D'ÉTAT

Source gallica.bnf.fr / Bibliothèque

6 April 1725
Born in Morosaglia, Corsica

1741
Enlists as a cadet in the Corsican Regiment at Naples

1752
Given a commission as second-lieutenant and transfers to Longone in Tuscany for garrison duty

1754
Elected leader of the Corsican independence movement

1755
Returns to Corsica to take part in revolt against the Republic of Genoa

1755
Elected General of the Corsicans

1755
Proclamation of the Corsican Republic with a Constitution inspired by Rousseau

1762
Consulta (assembly) convoked at Corte

1767
French invasion of Corsica

1768
Treaty of Genoa transfers Corsica to France

1769
Battle of Ponte Nuovo ends Corsican independence

1769
Flees to England where he lives in exile

1769
Birth of Nabuleone Buonaparte (15 August)

1789
National Assembly invites Paoli to Paris. He swears an oath of loyalty to the king and the Assembly

1790
Returns to Corsica

1793
Corsica secedes from France

1794–96
Anglo-Corsican Kingdom

1795
Flees Corsica (October)

1796
Corsica returns to French rule

1797
Arrives in England

5 February 1807
Dies in London

PASQUALE DI PAOLI

Pasquale Paoli was the second son of a prominent leader of the Corsican independence movement, Giacinto Paoli. On 15 July 1754, he was elected the leader of a Corsican revolt against the Republic of Genoa, which had ruled over Corsica since the thirteenth century. Paoli was just 30 years of age and was at the time serving as an officer in the army of Naples. He had spent the last 15 years in exile but Corsica was never far from his thoughts. The return of Paoli to the island represents a decisive phase in the Corsican struggle for independence. Not only was he able to give the movement an ideological grounding through the adoption of a 'Constitution' based on a number of 'universal principles', he was also able to gain international recognition for Corsica's standing. As a result, Paoli became by far the most prestigious leader of the Corsican independence movement.

Politically astute, eloquent, charming, widely read, of distinguished appearance and possessing a serenity that impressed contemporaries, he was also able to inspire in some of his countrymen a religious devotion bordering on the fanatical. The French bought the island from the Genoese in 1769, and then sent in the army to reclaim it. A decisive clash between the Corsican rebels and the French took place at Ponte Nuovo on 8 May 1769, when the rebels were decisively routed. Within a week most of the island was in French hands and even though sporadic fighting continued for a number of years to come, effective resistance was over. Paoli fled, eventually to England, and did not return to Corsica until after the French Revolution.

In the mind of the young Bonaparte, Paoli was a hero of the Corsican independence movement. Things turned sour, however, when Napoleon as a Jacobin revolutionary returned from France in 1791 and got himself elected as an officer in the Corsican National Guard; he soon clashed with Paoli over the direction of the Revolution. Paoli was a Corsican nationalist, while Napoleon sided with the French republicans. The execution of Louis XVI in 1793 was a turning point: Paoli split from France, throwing in his lot with the royalist party. Napoleon and his family remained loyal to France and had to flee Corsica as political refugees. Paoli then appealed to the British for help and for a while he was living under what was referred to as the Anglo-Corsican Kingdom. When the British withdrew their support in October 1795, Paoli had little choice but to follow the British into exile.

Philip Dwyer

CORONATION

the 30-second history

Napoleon's coronation, on

2 December 1804, was like no other ceremony the French had seen. Presided over by Pope Pius VII, who had travelled all the way from Rome expressly for the purpose, the ceremony took place in the cathedral of Notre Dame in Paris, and not in Rheims as tradition would have it, and was a mixture of religious, republican and *ancien-régime* symbolism that was meant to link the new Bonaparte dynasty to the ancient kings of France and, in particular, the Frankish ruler, Charlemagne. The pope anointed Napoleon, but the latter placed the crown on his own head. Then it was Josephine's turn. She knelt at Napoleon's feet – a gesture that signified she was subordinate to him – while Napoleon took the imperial diadem and placed it, again as planned, on his wife's head. This self-coronation broadcast the defining features of Napoleonic power. It was not the first time a sovereign had crowned himself, but in Napoleon's case it was meant to assuage Republican fears of too direct a rapprochement with the Vatican, as well as embodying the claim that as the supreme representative of the people Napoleon was the only person who could effect the transition from republic to empire.

RELATED TOPIC
See also
JOSEPHINE
page 36

3-SECOND SHOT
The coronation of Napoleon brought the French Revolution full circle: ten years after the execution of Louis XVI and the proclamation of a republic, Napoleon founded an empire.

3-MINUTE CODE
There was nothing terribly unusual about a European sovereign crowning his wife. In France, however, this was the first time that an empress had been anointed and crowned, and the first time in French history that a queen had been crowned at the same time as her male counterpart.

3-SECOND BIOGRAPHY
POPE PIUS VII
1742–1823
Born Barnaba Chiaramonti, Pius VII was consecrated on 14 March 1800, and endured a tumultuous relationship with Napoleon that eventually saw the pontiff deposed and imprisoned

30-SECOND TEXT
Philip Dwyer

Napoleon's coronation was a moment of great symbolism whose chief message was the definitive subordination of the Church to the temporal power.

MARIE-LOUISE

the 30-second history

The daughter of Francis I of

Austria, Marie-Louise had little education and was taught to hate both the French and Napoleon. That said, when Napoleon divorced Josephine, she became a natural candidate for his hand and was promised him in marriage in the hope that this would secure Austria's faltering international position. Not consulted about the match beforehand, she was yet swept off her feet by him and in March 1811, gave him a son and heir, Napoleon II, titled the King of Rome. Aided perhaps by Marie-Louise's sensuous nature, the marriage appears to have been one built on friendship and deep affection, Napoleon becoming a devoted family man and writing many love letters while he was away on campaign (though these were never as passionate as those he wrote to Josephine). In 1813, and again in 1814, Marie-Louise was made regent but she was able to do little to check the slide in the Empire's fortunes. Meanwhile, after leaving for the army to conduct the defence of France, Napoleon never saw her again: to his great sadness Marie-Louise refused to join him either on Elba in 1814 or in Paris in 1815. After the Congress of Vienna made her Duchess of Parma, Marie-Louise ruled there until her death in 1847.

RELATED TOPIC
See also
JOSEPHINE
page 36

3-SECOND SHOT
Napoleon's second wife, Princess Marie-Louise of Austria, was given to him, aged 18, in the hope that their marriage would secure Austria's place in Napoleonic Europe.

3-MINUTE CODE
European monarchies were tightly bound by blood links, and through marriage to an Austrian princess, Napoleon hoped he would be admitted into this 'society of princes'. This strategy proved a failure, however, the Emperor forever remaining the relative that everyone tolerates but no one likes.

3-SECOND BIOGRAPHIES
FRANCIS I OF AUSTRIA
1768–1835
Initially styled Francis II of the Holy Roman Empire, Francis I of Austria was a deeply cautious individual who loathed war and wanted to live at peace with Napoleon

NAPOLEON II
1811–32
Napoleon's son by Marie-Louise, Napoleon II was taken away from France in 1814 and lived out the rest of his life in Austria where he was given the title Duke of Reichstadt

30-SECOND TEXT
Philip Dwyer

Marry her for dynastic reasons though he did, Napoleon fell deeply in love with Marie-Louise, and was hurt by her refusal to have anything to do with him after 1814.

...omphe de Marie-Louise Imperatrice des Franç

ABDICATION

the 30-second history

The spring of 1814 saw Napoleon

in desperate trouble. Following the Battle of Leipzig, Austrian, Prussian and Russian armies had invaded France in overwhelming numbers, and a series of brilliant marches and counter-marches had failed to save Paris from occupation. Desperate to put an end to the fighting, on 6 April Napoleon's marshals forced him to issue a declaration stating that he would vacate the throne. To this day argument rages as to whether the marshals were justified. According to admirers of the Emperor, the latter was on the brink of a triumphant offensive that would have driven the invaders from Paris, whereas detractors of the Emperor believe that his cause was doomed and that the war had to be ended come what may. At all events the populace was desperate for peace and the regime's functionaries unwilling to administer its will. When peace came, there was therefore a general sense of relief, while the Allies' restoration of Louis XVIII met with no resistance. Only in parts of the army was there real lamentation, as witness the tearful scenes when Napoleon took leave of his Imperial Guard at Fontainebleau. Hence the military coup that brought him to power again in 1815, only to have to abdicate once again following the Battle of Waterloo.

3-SECOND SHOT
Napoleon abdicated twice, both times initially in favour of his son, Napoleon II, once in 1814, and once in 1815.

3-MINUTE CODE
By April 1814 Napoleon's cause was lost: conscription, administration and taxation had all broken down, while his senior commanders would no longer fight for him. With the army dwindling away to nothing due to disease, desertion and losses in battle, there was no option but surrender. However, Napoleon subsequently depicted himself as a tragic figure, betrayed by all those around him.

RELATED TOPICS
See also
EXILE
page 48

LEIPZIG
page 106

3-SECOND BIOGRAPHY
JEAN-BAPTISTE LYNCH
1749–1835
A prominent Bordeaux lawyer, Lynch was appointed mayor of his native city in 1808, but, like many other members of the propertied classes, he came to despair of Napoleon, and in 1814 opened the gates of the city to the oncoming troops of the Duke of Wellington

30-SECOND TEXT
Philip Dwyer

Brought to power by one military coup in 1799, Napoleon was overthrown by another in 1814 resulting in his first abdication.

EXILE

the 30-second history

After Napoleon's abdication in April 1814, he was formally ceded the island of Elba, off the Tuscan coast, with a pension of six million francs, and allowed to keep the title of emperor. However, faced by rumours that he was going to be removed, Napoleon decided to retake the throne, only to be defeated at Waterloo and banished to St Helena, a remote outpost in the South Atlantic. Installed high above Jamestown with a small entourage in a rundown villa called Longwood, Napoleon adopted the tactic of complaining about everything in the hope of getting back to Europe, but he also had much to complain about: the island's governor, Sir Hudson Lowe, refused to call him anything other than General Buonaparte, and generally made life on the island very uncomfortable. Meanwhile, many of Napoleon's servants and other followers were either removed by Lowe or found an excuse to leave: the word most used by contemporaries to describe St Helena was 'boredom'. At first Napoleon occupied his mind by dictating his memoirs, but they were more or less completed by 1819, and from then on his health deteriorated until he passed away on 5 May 1821, the autopsy showing that he died of a perforated duodenal ulcer that was becoming cancerous.

RELATED TOPIC
See also
ABDICATION
page 46

3-SECOND SHOT
Napoleon was exiled twice, first to the island of Elba after his first abdication in 1814, and then to the island of St Helena after his second abdication in 1815.

3-MINUTE CODE
Always possessed of an eye to posterity, Napoleon dictated his memoirs to four acolytes, the Count de Las Cases, General Gaspard Gourgaud, Count Bertrand and the Marquis of Montholon, the most famous of the works that resulted being Las Cases' *Memorial of Saint Helena*. Published in 1822, this contributed significantly to the transformation of an ogre, responsible for the deaths of millions, to a liberal emperor.

3-SECOND BIOGRAPHY
EMMANUEL DE LAS CASES
1765–1842
A sometime *émigré* who rallied to Napoleon and secured a position in the imperial household, Las Cases refused to abandon him in 1815 and made his fortune by recording his table-talk

30-SECOND TEXT
Philip Dwyer

There is no Battle of St Helena listed on the Arc de Triomphe, yet the island was the scene of Napoleon's greatest victory, namely the conquest of history in his memoirs.

MÉMORIAL
DE
SAINTE-HÉLÈNE
PAR LE Cte DE LAS CASES

DE NAPOLÉON DANS L'EXIL

EMPIRE ◑

ancien régime Also referred to as the 'Old Order', the *ancien régime* is a term used to describe the political and social situation of continental Europe prior to the French Revolution, its chief characteristics being absolute monarchy and the survival of both corporate privilege and various forms of feudalism.

Batavian Republic A satellite state that was established in Holland by the French in 1795, the Batavian Republic survived until it was transformed into a kingdom under Louis Bonaparte in 1806.

Bourbon Restoration Depending on the context, the term 'Bourbon restoration' refers either to the restoration of the Bourbon dynasty to the throne of France following the abdication of Napoleon in 1814 or to the regime that ruled France in the wake of this event.

Brabant Revolution A revolt that broke out in the then Austrian Netherlands (the western part of modern-day Belgium) in protest at the reformist policies of the Emperor Joseph II. Though suppressed without difficulty by the Austrians the following year, its red, yellow and black flag survived to become the flag of the independent Kingdom of Belgium in 1831.

Cisalpine Republic Centred on the Po valley with its capital at Milan, the Cisalpine Republic was one of a series of satellite states created by the victorious French armies in the period 1795–8. Its flag survived to provide the basis of the present-day Italian tricolour.

Confederation of the Rhine The Confederation of the Rhine was essentially a device made use of by Napoleon to secure his hegemony in Germany, a region of Europe that he regarded as strategically essential. In brief, as well as setting up a federal assembly, the rulers of the middling and small German states agreed to a perpetual offensive and defensive military alliance both with one another and with France.

Continental System The term 'Continental System' has two meanings. Properly speaking, it refers to the power-bloc created by Napoleon, namely a collection of dependent territories and satellite states that were to a greater or lesser extent in thrall to the will of Paris and intended to function as a source of raw materials and captive market. However, some scholars continue to use its older meaning, namely the trade embargo established by Napoleon as a means of bankrupting Britain and forcing her out of the war.

départements The *départements* (literally 'departments') were new units of local government set up in place of France's traditional provinces in the wake of the French Revolution. Roughly equal in size, they were invariably named after their chief geographical feature, and were copied in many of France's allies and satellite states.

émigrés The word *émigré* means 'emigrant', and in the context of the French Revolution refers to the many thousands who fled abroad rather than live under the new regime.

Habsburg Empire Often known simply as Austria on account of the fact that its capital was Vienna, in 1800 the Habsburg Empire was actually an extensive collection of territories including modern-day Austria, Hungary, the Czech Republic, Slovakia, Slovenia and Croatia, together with further areas of land in Germany, Italy, Poland and Serbia.

lycées Selective secondary schools established by Napoleon to provide the personnel needed to run the French Empire.

Risorgimento Literally 'the resurgence': the term given to the unification of Italy in the period 1859–70.

The Terror Unleashed in the summer of 1793 in the face of the renewed threats of foreign invasion, the Terror was a ruthless campaign designed to root out agents of counter-revolution and force the French populace to support the war effort that cost the lives of at least 20,000 people, including, most famously, Marie-Antoinette.

FRANCE

the 30-second history

Napoleon owed his rise to the

French Revolution and, in particular, to the campaigns he waged on its behalf. He never doubted his debt to France and insisted that he respected her interests at all times; and at first sight, France did very well from him. As First Consul and, later, Emperor, he extended French hegemony across Europe, gathered tributes from occupied territories, and filled the Louvre with plundered works of art, whilst the economic system he imposed was primarily designed to benefit French commerce and industry, often at the expense of his allies. Yet Napoleon was not just a great leader in war, but also a domestic reformer who built on the innovations of the French Revolution and gave France solid administrative and judicial structures, his domestic legacy including the introduction of prefects and sub-prefects in every department, the famous civil code, the Concordat with the Catholic Church and a state system of *lycées* and higher education. At the same time, the turbulence of the Revolutionary decade was brought to an end. However, by 1814 France was exhausted, ground down by conscription, requisitions and the demands of endless war: hence the rapid collapse of the regime in the face of foreign invasion.

3-SECOND SHOT
Napoleon always put France's interests first: he sought to create a French Empire that would rival the past empires of ancient Rome and of Charlemagne.

3-MINUTE CODE
Napoleon appealed to a desire for military glory that was especially strong among his soldiers. Nothing else can explain his success in 1815, after escaping from exile in Elba, in winning them over for a new campaign. That campaign ended in defeat at Waterloo and a second exile, on St Helena. But Napoleon's appeal lived on: his nephew Louis-Napoleon Bonaparte would be elected president in 1848 before seizing power as Emperor in 1851.

RELATED TOPICS
See also
THE CIVIL CODE
page 140

THE CONCORDAT
page 142

CONSCRIPTION
page 144

3-SECOND BIOGRAPHY
LOUIS-NAPOLEON
BONAPARTE
1808–73
Napoleon's nephew and heir to a Bonapartist tradition that lived on for much of the nineteenth century, Louis-Napoleon was elected President of the Second Republic in 1848 before staging his own military coup and taking the title of Emperor Napoleon III in 1851

30-SECOND TEXT
Alan Forrest

Napoleon always claimed that he represented the interests of France in his own person: whether this belief was genuine or not, the truth was very different.

PROCLAMATION
L'EMPEREUR

BELGIUM

the 30-second history

The state now known as Belgium

was not born until 1830. In the late eighteenth century it had been an integral part of the Habsburg Empire, and was one of the first areas to be taken over by France: aiming to establish natural frontiers to the north and east, between 1792 and 1795 French troops fought to make Belgium an integral part of the French Republic. Formally annexed to France in 1797, it was divided into French-style *départements*, bringing French administration and justice closer to the people. Together with the introduction of conscription, this was met with anger and open revolt in large parts of Brabant and Flanders in 1798. The rebellion was soon put down, but public opinion was not won over and by 1800 Belgium had produced no more than a quarter of its quota of recruits. Thereafter, Napoleonic rule did help to expand a number of sectors of the Belgian economy, but it still failed to make the population feel French, arousing resentment through tighter policing, higher taxes and the constant demands for fresh troops. Since the local élites showed no more eagerness to serve the Empire than they had the Habsburgs, the prefects, too, were largely French. This meant that imperial government was imposed rather than consensual.

3-SECOND SHOT
Napoleon failed to win over the Belgian public, even in French-speaking Wallonia, and there was little dismay when the Empire was dissolved in 1814.

3-MINUTE CODE
Napoleon's career was destined to end in Belgium, where he fought his last battle, at Waterloo, in 1815. For the Belgians the battlefield would become a *lieu de mémoire*, a place future generations could visit where Napoleon's imperial dream was finally dashed. Its most famous monument, the Lion Mound, was erected by the Dutch in 1826 to commemorate their military contribution to Napoleon's downfall and to celebrate their own hero, William, Prince of Orange.

RELATED TOPIC
See also
WATERLOO
page 108

3-SECOND BIOGRAPHIES
JEAN-BAPTISTE DUMONCEAU
1760–1821
One of at least 25 Belgians who served as generals in Napoleon's army, Dumonceau began his military career in the forces of the Brabant Revolution of 1790 and afterwards fled to France where he enlisted in the army, eventually securing the rank of General of Division and the title of Count of Bergendal

WILLIAM, PRINCE OF ORANGE
1792–1849
Crown Prince of the Netherlands after his father was crowned William I in 1815. He led I Corps in Wellington's Anglo-Dutch army at Waterloo and became a hero of the Orangist cause

30-SECOND TEXT
Alan Forrest

The scene of France's first conquests in 1792, Belgium was also the scene of its final eradication in 1815.

HOLLAND

the 30-second history

Holland had a turbulent history

in the years following the Batavian Revolution of 1795 which turned it into a sister republic of revolutionary France. Reborn first as the Batavian Republic, then as the Batavian Commonwealth, Holland was of particular interest to Napoleon because of its commercial wealth, its strategic position and the strength of its navy. In 1806 it was formed into the Kingdom of Holland under his brother Louis, who was given autocratic powers and the task of supplying taxes and conscripts for the war effort. Louis worked hard to prove himself to his subjects through constitutional and fiscal reform, local government reorganization and a consolidation of state finances. But the Dutch were a commercial people with a long constitutional history of their own, and he struggled to win them over. More critically, Napoleon regarded Louis as too ready to put Dutch interests above those of the Empire, and insufficiently ruthless in imposing the Continental Blockade. In 1810 he abruptly removed Louis from the throne, and, while technically Louis had abdicated in favour of his second son, Napoleon did not recognize the succession. Instead he abolished the Kingdom, annexing it to the Empire and dividing its territory into nine French-style *départements*. From 1810 to 1814 all pretence of Dutch independence was abandoned.

RELATED TOPICS
See also
CONTINENTAL BLOCKADE
page 98

SIBLINGS
page 150

3-SECOND SHOT
Under Napoleon Holland became a kingdom under his brother Louis, then, when Louis showed too much independence, the kingdom was abolished and Holland annexed directly.

3-MINUTE CODE
With their strong administrative and judicial traditions the Dutch were among the most governable subjects of the Empire. However, discontent over requisitions, conscription and the Continental System remained rife, and as Napoleon's military advances were reversed in Russia and at Leipzig, there were uprisings against his regime in Holland. There were few signs of regret when, after 1813, Holland was liberated from Napoleonic rule.

3-SECOND BIOGRAPHY
ISAAC GOGEL
1765–1821
Amsterdam merchant of strongly democratic and reformist views who twice became Minister of Finance in the Batavian Republic and went on to serve Louis Bonaparte in the same capacity with considerable success

30-SECOND TEXT
Alan Forrest

In some respects one of the more settled parts of the Napoleonic Empire, Holland was nonetheless quick to break away from French rule when opportunity finally offered in 1814.

2 February 1754
Born in Paris

1770
Enters the seminary of
Saint-Sulpice

1779
Ordained to the
priesthood

1788
Named Bishop of Autun

1789
Elected to the Estates-
General as deputy of the
clergy of Autun; crosses
over to the Third Estate

1790
Takes the oath to the
Civil Constitution of
the Clergy

1792
Order issued for his arrest
as an *émigré*

1793
Flees to Philadelphia

1796
Returns to France after
absence of four years

1797
Appointed Minister of
Foreign Affairs under
the Directory

1799
Appointed Foreign
Minister by the Consulate

1804
Named Grand Chamberlain
under the Empire

1805
Receives Legion
of Honour

1807
Resigns as Foreign
Minister

1813
Refuses Napoleon's
offer of Ministry of
Foreign Affairs

1814
Elected president of the
Provisional Government
and signs armistice with
the Allies

1815
Signs Declaration against
Napoleon at the Congress
of Vienna

1830
Appointed French
ambassador to London

1831
Signs treaty fixing new
borders for Belgium

17 May 1838
Dies in Paris

CHARLES DE TALLEYRAND

The man who would be principal foreign policy adviser to Napoleon had a long and colourful career. Born into an aristocratic family from Périgord in southwest France, Charles-Maurice de Talleyrand-Périgord studied for the priesthood and was appointed Bishop of Autun in 1788, on the eve of the French Revolution – a revolution he instinctively supported. He was elected to the Estates-General as representative of the clergy of Autun, and soon found himself helping to draft France's new constitution and voting for the Civil Constitution of the Clergy. He resigned his see in 1791 and consigned himself to politics, serving almost every regime during the revolutionary and Napoleonic era. Only during the Terror did he abandon public office and go into exile – first in Britain, then in the United States – which resulted in his being listed as an *émigré*. After he returned to France in 1796 he was seldom out of the public eye, and would prove himself a consummate diplomat in the service of his country.

Talleyrand served as foreign minister from 1797 under the Directory, yet he also helped plan the coup that brought Napoleon to power. Under the Consulate he again had responsibility for foreign diplomacy, and he was especially influential in easing France's relations with the Papacy. After 1804 he continued to serve Napoleon as Emperor, though he was increasingly critical of Napoleon's continual wars, and especially of the decision to invade Spain. From 1807 he was out of office and had little influence on Napoleon's decision-making; and after the disaster of the Russian Campaign he shrewdly turned down the offer of returning to his service. By 1813 he was conspiring with the Bourbons, and in 1814 was appointed France's principal representative at the Congress of Vienna, where he is widely credited for gaining exceptionally favourable terms for his country. During the Hundred Days he remained on the side of the Bourbon Restoration.

Talleyrand was undoubtedly a first-rate diplomat, but few trusted him. Between 1789 and 1815 he served every regime except the Jacobin Republic: he seemed equally at ease working for the Revolution, the Empire and the Bourbon monarchy, and did not hesitate to betray them when it was in his interest to do so. His was an exceptional political career, stretching over four decades. One of his last diplomatic achievements, indeed, was his role in the creation of a Belgian state following the Revolution of 1830.

Alan Forrest

GERMANY

the 30-second history

German Central Europe – the lands

that lay to the east of France that had been at the heart of the Carolingian Empire which he dreamt of recreating – was always critical to Napoleon's imperial ambitions. Germany, of course, did not yet exist as a political entity. It was a patchwork of kingdoms and electorates, of which the most powerful were Prussia in the north and Austria, itself the hub of a multinational empire, in the south. Inheriting the determination of earlier regimes to extend France's frontiers to the Rhine – a desire fulfilled by the Republic's annexation of Belgium and the Rhineland – Napoleon went further, encouraging the middle-sized states to swallow up the smaller territories around them and transforming them into satellite kingdoms. Having defeated the Austrians in 1805, he dissolved the thousand-year-old Holy Roman Empire, and replaced it with the new Confederation of the Rhine, thereby inaugurating an era of widespread political, social and economic reform. However, despite the failure of a number of attempts to stir up popular revolts in 1809, French rule was not popular in much of Germany, and the Emperor therefore received little backing when the German princes turned against him in the wake of the Battle of Leipzig.

3-SECOND SHOT
Napoleon's greatest victories were won in Germany, yet it was his losses in Germany in 1813 which, more than any, destroyed his imperial ambitions.

3-MINUTE CODE
If Napoleon was seen by many Germans as a usurper who had occupied much of their homeland, he was accredited by others with modernizing the state. In the wake of the Battle of Jena, Prussia reformed her political institutions and restructured her army with resounding success, while German nationalism was boosted by anti-Napoleonic fervour, ushering in a new era in German history. 'In the beginning', said the German historian Thomas Nipperdey, 'was Napoleon.'

RELATED TOPICS
See also
JENA-AUERSTÄDT
page 82

LEIPZIG
page 106

3-SECOND BIOGRAPHY
MAXIMILIAN VON MONTGELAS
1759–1838
An official of distinctly radical opinions, Montgelas became chief minister of Bavaria in 1799 and thereafter pursued a policy of territorial aggrandizement and domestic reform whose keystone was friendship with the France of Napoleon Bonaparte

30-SECOND TEXT
Alan Forrest

Germany being the essential keystone of the Napoleonic Empire, its loss in 1813 made the Emperor's defeat inevitable.

ITALY

the 30-second history

Napoleon's military reputation had been built during the Italian campaign of 1796–97. As such, although the region was important for strategic reasons, it is no surprise that in 1805 he had himself crowned King of Italy (though, in fact, the area involved was limited to the territories of the erstwhile Cisalpine Republic, augmented though these later were by Venetia and the South Tyrol). As a Corsican, Napoleon felt a special bond with Italy. He felt he understood the Italian people, knowing those circumstances where he could rely on the Italian élites to provide leadership and governance and those where he had to turn to Frenchmen, including, not least, his stepson, Eugène de Beauharnais, who was entrusted with the viceroyalty of the Kingdom of Italy. Setting aside this last state, most of the north of the country was tightly integrated into his Empire, Piedmont, Genoa, Parma, Piacenza, Tuscany and Rome all being directly annexed to France. Mainland Naples, meanwhile, was occupied and transformed into a satellite kingdom under, first, Joseph Bonaparte (1806–8), and, second, Joachim Murat (1806–15), and Tuscany, Lucca and Piombino given to Napoleon's sister, Elise. All this was accompanied by massive reform: across Italy French administration and justice were imposed, feudalism abolished and the Church stripped of much of its land.

3-SECOND SHOT
In the nineteenth century many in Italy looked on the Napoleonic period as the dawn of a new era, the period of national unification known as the Risorgimento.

3-MINUTE CODE
The Napoleonic period occupies a position of enormous importance in the history of Italy. Although his exile on St Helena saw the Emperor claim that his final goal was the unification of the country, no progress was made in this respect in geographical terms. However, nationalism was greatly stimulated, while the social, administrative and economic reforms implemented by the French and their collaborators (many of which survived after 1815) paved the way for future economic growth.

RELATED TOPIC
See also
MARENGO
page 76

3-SECOND BIOGRAPHIES
MICHELE PEZZA
1771–1806
Generally known by his nom d'guerre of 'Fra Diavolo' because of his reputation for ferocity, Pezza was a prominent leader of the widespread irregular resistance which the French and their supporters faced in southern Italy in 1799 and then again in 1806–11

GUGLIELMO PEPE
1783–1855
An officer in the Neapolitan army, Pepe was typical of the thousands of young Italians who were inspired by the Napoleonic experience to dream of a free and united Italy, and therefore came to play a prominent part in revolutionary politics in Italy after 1814

30-SECOND TEXT
Alan Forrest

Ably ruled by Eugène de Beauharnais, Napoleon's stepson, th[e] Kingdom of Italy was a model satellite state.

POLAND

the 30-second history

Napoleon's invasion of Poland,

following his military humiliation of Prussia in 1806, has a unique place in the history of the Empire. His troops were welcomed as liberators by local people, who staged a popular uprising in his support. The Polish élite rushed to offer their services to their new ruler and to the state he created, the Grand Duchy of Warsaw, though its very existence led to further conflict in central and eastern Europe, notably with Russia in 1812. Napoleon has enjoyed a good press in Poland. He had publicly declared his admiration for the Poles back in the 1790s, and he famously had a Polish lover in Countess Maria Walewska. But he was ruthless in exploiting the Grand Duchy for his own ends, for taxes, horses and military supplies. In particular he turned to Poland for conscripts: over 100,000 Polish soldiers died fighting for the Grande Armée in the years to 1814. Yet many Poles afterwards refused to see his rule as exploitation, welcoming his intervention as an opportunity for self-government after the partitions of 1772, 1793 and 1795 that had divided the lands of the Polish-Lithuanian Commonwealth between Austria, Prussia and Russia.

RELATED TOPICS

See also
FRIEDLAND
page 86

RUSSIA
page 104

LEIPZIG
page 106

LOUIS DAVOUT
page 114

3-SECOND SHOT
Many Poles in the nineteenth century continued to look back on Napoleon's Grand Duchy of Warsaw as the foundation stone of an independent Polish state.

3-MINUTE CODE
The Napoleonic period is still remembered in Poland today. The Polish national anthem is the marching-song of the Polish Legion (a force raised in northern Italy from Polish soldiers taken by the French while serving in the Austrian army by Jan Henryk Dabrowski). As well as calling on Dabrowski to liberate Poland, the words specifically identify Napoleon with Polish patriotism. 'We shall be Polish', it declares; 'Bonaparte has given us the example of how we should prevail.'

3-SECOND BIOGRAPHY
JAN HENRYK DABROWSKI
1755–1818
A general in the Polish army who fled into exile after the third partition of Poland in 1795 and thereafter devoted his life to the restoration of the Polish state, next to fellow general Tadeuz Kosciuszko, Dabrowski remains Poland's greatest national hero

30-SECOND TEXT
Alan Forrest

Known as the Grand Duchy of Warsaw, the satellite state created by Napoleon in Poland gave the Emperor many thousands of soldiers

SPAIN

the 30-second history

Napoleon's intervention in Spain

in 1808 seemed to promise much: the Spanish government was in disarray, the army and navy very weak, and the whole country in crisis. But his decision to take over proved rash: though he managed to put his brother Joseph on the throne, the latter's authority was immediately challenged by a massive insurrection that led directly to the Peninsular War of 1808–14. This did not push reform into the background, however. On the contrary, Napoleon clearly saw it as a useful way of mobilizing Spanish support, and in 1808 both drew up a constitution and promulgated a series of decrees whose chief target was the religious orders. Meanwhile, further measures were drawn up by the Spanish administration formed by Joseph Bonaparte, the most notable being the division of the country into French-style *départements*. Yet all this came to nought. Spanish resistance was never overcome; the commanders of the French forces refused to respect Joseph Bonaparte's authority; money for such innovations as a system of state secondary schools on the French model was non-existent; the few Spanish troops whom Joseph managed to raise deserted as fast as they could be uniformed; and Napoleon failed to give Joseph the sort of backing he needed to turn good intentions into reality.

3-SECOND SHOT
Napoleon intervened in Spain to impose political stability and ensure that the country played its full part in the Napoleonic enterprise; in both goals he was to be frustrated.

3-MINUTE CODE
The Peninsular War is chiefly remembered as an ugly conflict scarred by savage guerrilla attacks and horrific acts of revenge carried out on the civilian population, but this perception is now increasingly challenged, while the French genuinely believed themselves to be engaged in a civilizing mission. In present-day Spain, meanwhile, the decision to resist Napoleon is frequently seen as a historic error that retarded national development for many years.

RELATED TOPICS
See also
PENINSULAR WAR
page 100

ARTHUR WELLESLEY, 1ST DUKE OF WELLINGTON
page 102

JEAN-DE-DIEU SOULT
page 126

SIBLINGS
page 150

3-SECOND BIOGRAPHY
FRANCISCO GOYA Y LUCIENTE
1746–1828
Spanish court's chief painter prior to 1808. Goya portrayed the Peninsular War as very much a conflict between the Spanish people and the French army as well as one characterized by horrors of every sort.

30-SECOND TEXT
Alan Forrest

Spain, along with Portugal, was the scene the Peninsular War, nex to the campaign in Russ by far the most dreadfu human experience of the Napoleonic epoch.

DE BAILEN

BATALLA DE BAILEN

VICTORIES

Battle of Aspern-Essling Fought on 21 and 22 May 1809 outside Vienna when a large Austrian army commanded by the Archduke Charles frustrated a French attempt to cross the Danube, the Battle of Aspern-Essling was Napoleon's first defeat.

Cisalpine Republic Centred on the Po valley with its capital at Milan, the Cisalpine Republic was one of a series of satellite states created by the victorious French armies in the period 1795–8. Its flag survived to provide the basis of the present-day Italian tricolour.

Confederation of the Rhine The Confederation of the Rhine was essentially a device made use of by Napoleon to secure his hegemony in Germany, a region of Europe that he regarded as strategically essential. In brief, as well as setting up a federal assembly, the rulers of the middling and small German states agreed to a perpetual offensive and defensive military alliance both with one another and with France.

Coup of 18 Brumaire A date in the new calendar adopted by the newly formed French Republic in 1792 that corresponds to 9 November, 18 Brumaire was the day in 1799 when a Napoleon freshly returned from Egypt seized power in Paris with the help of the army.

Grande Armée Literally 'grand army' or 'big army'. Properly speaking, the army commanded by Napoleon himself in the campaigns of 1805–14. However, the term is sometimes used as a synonym for the army of Napoleon as a whole.

The Hundred Days The Hundred Days is the term generally given to the brief period in 1815 when Napoleon resumed power in France following his escape from Elba.

le manoeuvre sur les derrières A favourite operational device of Napoleon's, the _manoeuvre sur les derrières_ or, in English, 'manoeuvre upon the rear' involved bypassing an enemy army and then swinging round so as to take it from behind.

Old Guard A conglomerate of units that was the senior element of Napoleon's Imperial Guard and included several units of infantry and cavalry. Of these, by far the most famous was the Grenadiers à Pied de la Garde Imperiale.

Peace of Tilsit Signed in July 1807, the peace of Tilsit saw Napoleon end hostilities with Prussia and Russia in the wake of his crushing victory over the Russians at Friedland. In brief, Prussia was treated with great harshness and stripped of half her territory, but Russia escaped scot-free, Napoleon seeing her as a potential partner in his war with Britain.

Prussia The most powerful of the 365 states into which modern-day Germany was divided in 1800, with the exception of the break constituted by the smaller state of Hanover, Prussia stretched from the River Rhine to the frontiers of Russia and enjoyed a great military reputation thanks to the victories of Frederick II. Humiliated by Napoleon in 1806 in the campaign of Jena and Auerstädt, she later recovered and went on to play a key role in his downfall.

Treaty of Pressburg Signed by Austria in the wake of the disastrous campaign of October–December 1805, the Treaty of Pressburg forced her to pay a large indemnity and stripped her not only of all the territory she had obtained from the Republic of Venice via the Treaty of Campo Formio, but the Alpine territory of the Tyrol too.

War of the First Coalition A conflict that broke out in 1792 and lasted till 1797, the War of the First Coalition saw a range of European states take arms against the French Revolution, only to be forced, one by one, to make peace.

War of the Second Coalition Provoked by Napoleon's invasion of Egypt in 1798, the War of the Second Coalition saw Russia, Austria, Turkey and Naples join Britain in attempting to restrict the power of France. Though the French were forced to surrender Egypt, elsewhere they were victorious, the conflict being brought to a close by the treaty of Amiens in May 1802.

Young Guard The most junior element of Napoleon's Imperial Guard and a late addition to its forces, the Young Guard saw much action in the campaigns of 1813–14 and was all but completely destroyed at the Battle of Waterloo.

ITALIAN CAMPAIGN

the 30-second history

3-SECOND SHOT
Speed, determination and
energy defined Napoleon's
campaign in Italy during
which, on chasing the
Austrians from Lombardy,
he remarked: 'They have
seen nothing yet.'

3-MINUTE CODE
Napoleon redrew the
map of Italy, establishing
the satellite Cisalpine
Republic and handing over
Venetia to Austria. In the
former strong local support
ensured the abolition
of feudalism, the opening
of the ghettos, the
dissolution of the guilds
and a general assault on
the Church. Meanwhile,
popular unrest was brutally
crushed. Napoleonic rule
continued until 1814,
ushering in the birth of
modern Italy.

Not least by employing what
became his hallmark strategies of the central
position and the *manoeuvre sur les derrières*,
Napoleon established a reputation as a dynamic
commander during his Italian campaign of
1796–7, in the course of which he overran
northern and central Italy, and compelled
Piedmont, Austria and the Papal States to
accept peace terms, thereby sounding the death
knell of the War of the First Coalition, making
him a popular hero in France and launching him
on the path to power. In brief, the campaign
can be divided into three phases. Striking north
from the area of Genoa in April 1796, Napoleon
defeated Piedmont in three weeks and took
Milan, but was then checked by the Austrian-
held fortress of Mantua which held out for many
months despite the defeat of four successive
attempts to relieve the siege. With Mantua
taken, Napoleon was able to resume the
offensive. Thus, having first forced the Papal
States to make peace, he overran the Venetian
Republic and marched on Vienna. With their
capital in danger, the Austrians signed an
armistice at Leoben, followed by a formal
treaty at Campo Formio. Of the First Coalition,
meanwhile, only Britain, Naples and Portugal
remained in the fight, the outlook being so
grim that even Britain opened peace talks.

RELATED TOPICS
See also
ANDRÉ MASSÉNA
page 118

ARMY
page 134

3-SECOND BIOGRAPHIES
DAGOBERT WURMSER
1724–97
An Austrian general defeated
by Napoleon at Castiglione,
Wurmser redeemed his
reputation by a nine-month
defence of Mantua

PIERRE AUGEREAU
1757–1816
A republican general and future
Marshal of France, Augereau
played a major part in the
French victories at Millesimo,
Lonato and Castiglione

30-SECOND TEXT
Frederick C. Schneid

*The real foundation of
Napoleon's prominence,
and a study in military
genius, the Italian
campaign was won
by speed and daring.*

BATTLE
OF
RIVOLI
14 & 15 January 1797

MARENGO

the 30-second history

Napoleon's victory at Marengo

was the turning point in the War of the Second Coalition (1798–1802). In 1799 an Austro-Russian army invaded Italy, overrunning the pro-French Cisalpine Republic. Disagreements in the coalition however, led to Russian withdrawal from the war, thereby allowing Napoleon to launch a counter-offensive in Italy in May 1800. Utilizing his strategy of *le manœuvre sur les derrières*, Napoleon crossed the Alps via the St Bernard Pass, captured Milan, thereby placing the French army behind the Austrian forces under General Melas in northwest Italy. With this objective secured, Napoleon marched against the main Austrian army at Alessandria. Believing the Austrians to be hiding behind the city walls, Napoleon dispersed his army, sending General Desaix south to block possible Austrian escape routes. Taking advantage of this situation, on 14 June Melas attacked Napoleon's army at Marengo. Badly outnumbered, the First Consul suffered heavy losses and was compelled to retreat. Hearing the distant sound of cannon, Desaix rushed to Napoleon's aid and counter-attacked at the head of his division. The Austrians fought hard, but were eventually defeated and compelled to seek an armistice. When war resumed in December, the French again defeated the Austrians, leading to their withdrawal from the coalition.

3-SECOND SHOT
Napoleon seemingly lost the Battle of Marengo in the morning, but won it by nightfall.

3-MINUTE CODE
The campaign of Marengo was more impressive than the battle fought to conclude it. A victim of over-confidence, the First Consul only held against Melas as long as he did because of the tactical inferiority of the Austrian army. Much embarrassed by his near reverse, Napoleon rewrote the official account of the battle so as to hide his defeat in the first part of the action.

RELATED TOPICS
See also
JEAN LANNES
page 116

JOACHIM MURAT
page 120

CLAUDE VICTOR PERRIN
page 128

ARMY
page 134

3-SECOND BIOGRAPHIES
MICHAEL, BARON MELAS
1729–1806
A highly experienced Austrian general, on 4 June 1800 Melas forced the surrender of Genoa after a long siege

LOUIS DESAIX
1768–1800
A talented French general of noble origins, Desaix served with distinction on the Rhine in 1795–7 and commanded a division in Egypt

30-SECOND TEXT
Frederick C. Schneid

Victory at Marengo solidified Napoleon's political power as First Consul.

AUSTERLITZ

the 30-second history

The Battle of Austerlitz on

2 December 1805 was Napoleon's most important and decisive victory. Since 1802, Napoleon's repeated and blatant violations of international borders in Italy and Germany had led to the formation of an anti-French coalition comprising Russia, Austria, Great Britain, Sweden and the Kingdom of Naples. Napoleon's response was a three-month campaign that took his army from the Channel coast to the Rhine River and into southern Germany. The rapid march of the French army led to the defeat and surrender of an Austrian army at Ulm, followed by the capture of Vienna. A Russian army under Kutuzov joined with Austrian forces 60 kilometres (40 miles) north of the city. Despite being outnumbered, Napoleon sought battle. Enticed to attack his right flank, the allies fell for the trap whereupon Napoleon attacked their centre, seizing the Pratzen Heights, and then defeating their troops piecemeal. Completely demoralized, the Russians returned home while the Austrians were compelled to sign a humiliating peace treaty at Pressburg three weeks later. With his reputation as a military genius established beyond dispute, Napoleon was now the arbiter of central Europe.

RELATED TOPICS
See also
LOUIS DAVOUT
page 114

JOACHIM MURAT
page 120

JEAN-DE-DIEU SOULT
page 126

ARMY
page 134

3-SECOND SHOT
The events of the 1805 campaign – the destruction of the enemy's main army and seizure of its capital – became the hallmark of Napoleonic conquest.

3-MINUTE CODE
Austerlitz transformed Europe. Austria was forced to pay for the war and cede territory to France's ally, Bavaria; Prussia entered an alliance with France; the Holy Roman Empire was abolished and replaced by Napoleon's Confederation of the Rhine; and a French army conquered Naples, leaving Napoleon master of Italy too. On the other hand, both Russia and Austria were persuaded to pursue military reforms that were one day to spell the end of French military superiority.

3-SECOND BIOGRAPHIES
MIKHAIL, PRINCE KUTUZOV
1745–1813
A disciple of Suvorov, Kutuzov opposed fighting at Austerlitz and went on to become the best-known Russian general of the Napoleonic Wars

KARL, BARON MACK
1752–1828
Chief of staff of the Austrian army in 1805, Mack favoured war with Napoleon but was defeated at Ulm

30-SECOND TEXT
Frederick C. Schneid

Known as the Battle of the Three Emperors, Austerlitz is often seen as Napoleon's greatest victory.

16 August 1776
Born at Drouyes-les-Belles Fontaines in the French department of the Yonne

1784
Runs away from home with his older brother

1799
Conscripted into the French army

1800
Captures Austrian cannon singlehandedly at Montebello

1801
Appointed Pioneer and serves with French army in the 'War of the Oranges'

1803
Appointed to the Consular Guard

1804
First private soldier awarded the Legion of Honour

1807
Promoted to Corporal

1809
Promoted to Sergeant

1812
Promoted to Lieutenant of the Grenadiers à pied de la Garde Imperiale

1813
Promoted to Captain and attached to Napoleon's headquarters

1814
Laid off on half-pay under Louis XVIII

1815
Rallies to Napoleon during the Hundred Days

1816
Again laid off on half-pay

1829
Officially retired from service after thirty years

10 December 1865
Dies

EAN-ROCH COIGNET

3orn in 1776, Jean-Roch Coignet ame from a poor family and ran away from ome at the age of eight, thereafter working as shepherd boy and farm labourer until he was onscripted into the French army in 1799. ssigned to the 96th Line, he participated in ne Coup of 18 Brumaire and a few months later ought in the Marengo campaign, displaying reat courage at Montebello, where he nglehandedly captured an Austrian cannon.

Promoted to the rank of pioneer as a reward or his bravery during the Italian campaign, oignet was next sent to Spain with the troops eployed there for the purpose of the short- ved 'War of the Oranges' of 1801 and remained ith his regiment until 1803, when he was fered an appointment to the Consular uard, an elite unit that became the famous renadiers of Napoleon's Imperial Guard in 304. When Napoleon established the Legion Honour, Coignet was also the first private oldier to receive this award.

As a decorated soldier in what soon became nown as the 'Old Guard' (a conglomerate of nits that included not just the Grenadiers of the Guard but also several other units of infantry and cavalry), Coignet served in all the major campaigns of the Napoleonic Wars and was at Austerlitz, Jena, Eylau, Friedland, Aspern-Essling and Wagram. A lieutenant at the time of the Russian campaign, he was among the 95,000 troops who reached Moscow and fought with the rear-guard in the subsequent retreat before rejoining Napoleon's new army in May 1813. Promoted to the rank of captain, he was appointed to Imperial Headquarters, and from this vantage point witnessed the battles of Lützen, Bautzen, Dresden, Leipzig and Hanau, as well as the campaign in France in 1814.

After Napoleon's abdication, Coignet was laid off on half pay. Having immediately rallied to the imperial banner when the Emperor escaped from Elba, during the Hundred Days he again served at Imperial Headquarters. Though kept under surveillance by the police until 1818, he was left free to marry and open a shop, and was not stripped of his military status altogether, technically remaining an officer in the French army until he officially retired after 30 years of military service in 1829.

Frederick C. Schneid

JENA–AUERSTÄDT

the 30-second history

The twin battles of Jena and Auerstädt, fought on 14 October 1806, resulted in catastrophe for Prussia. Frederick William III declared war on Napoleon after much French double-dealing and led his army southwards to attack the Grande Armée. Deploying the latter into three mutually supporting parallel columns, Napoleon manoeuvred around the flank of the Prussian forces and, two weeks after the campaign began, attacked them. Of the two battles Jena was the more easily gained as Napoleon's main army of 95,000 faced no more than 60,000 Prussians and Saxons. However, at Auerstädt, 20 kilometres (13 miles) to the north, Davout's 30,000-strong III Corps unexpectedly ran into the main Prussian army of 80,000 men and only triumphed after repelling repeated assaults, one of which cost the life of Brunswick, the Prussian commander. After the dual victories, a vigorous pursuit by the French led to the complete disintegration of the Prussian army and, with it, the collapse of the Prussian state. Entering Berlin a week later, Napoleon directed his forces east to engage a Russian army advancing through Poland. The campaign continued until the Peace of Tilsit in July 1807, when Prussia surrendered and Russia entered into an alliance with France.

3-SECOND SHOT
Napoleon outmanoeuvred, outgeneralled and outfought the Prussians at Jena and Auerstädt.

3-MINUTE CODE
Napoleon's rapid and decisive victory over Prussia enhanced his military reputation and consolidated his power in central Europe through the expansion of the Confederation of the Rhine and the creation of the Grand Duchy of Warsaw. Following Tilsit, meanwhile, Prussia lost half her territory and became a virtual French dependency. That said, the rapid collapse of the Prussian state led to significant civil and military reforms that paved the way for resurgence in 1813.

RELATED TOPICS
See also
LOUIS DAVOUT
page 114

JOACHIM MURAT
page 120

ARMY
page 134

3-SECOND BIOGRAPHIES
CHARLES WILLIAM FERDINAN
DUKE OF BRUNSWICK
1731–1806
Commander of the Prussian army in 1806, Brunswick is most famous for his decision not to attack the French at Valmy (20 September 1792)

HEINRICH, BARON VOM STE
1757–1831
A senior Prussian bureaucrat, Vom Stein became the chief figurehead of Prussian resistance to Napoleon after the battles of Jena and Auerstädt and initiated important reforms aimed at revivifying the Prussian state

30-SECOND TEXT
Frederick C. Schneid

For Prussia, Jena and Auerstädt represented complete humiliation.

Morseburg • Leipsic
Lucan
Naumburg •
Cambrug
Jena O Gera
Wiels
Mittel
Faabli
Auma
Jena O
Fulda
Chotia O Pława

Lisdorf
Hassenhausen

Sonnenberg

S. R. Sool

AUERSTÄDT.

Apolda
Stobra
Neckwitz
Kulabach
Lio Romstedt
Romsdorf
Vierzehn Heiligen
Borlberg
Gr. Romstedt
Sperlie Bon

EYLAU

the 30-second history

Napoleon won a pyrrhic victory

over the Russians at Eylau on 8 February 1807. After the occupation of Berlin in October 1806, Napoleon marched into Poland to engage the Russian army under Bennigsen. After much manoeuvring both armies settled into winter quarters in late December, but aggressive reconnaissance by Marshal Ney compelled the Russians to take the field afresh. After several smaller engagements, the Russian army stood at Eylau. Napoleon began the battle outnumbered 65,000 to 45,000. During the course of the day, however, Marshals Davout and Ney arrived on the flanks, thereby establishing numerical parity despite the arrival of L'Estocq's Prussians. In the midst of the battle, Augereau's VII Corps was caught in the face of massed Russian guns. The entire corps was decimated, leaving a gap in Napoleon's line. To shore up his position he dispatched Marshal Murat with the entire heavy cavalry reserve of 15,000 men. This force smashed into the Russian centre, buying time for the French to reorganize. By sunset, Napoleon's forces had seized the Russian positions, but at a heavy price while they were unable to prevent the Russians withdrawing from the field in good order. With combined casualties exceeding 50,000 men, Napoleon and Bennigsen were compelled to return to winter quarters.

3-SECOND SHOT
The bloody Battle of Eylau cost Napoleon precious manpower and denied him the decisive victory that he sought in the campaign he was then waging against Russia.

3-MINUTE CODE
Though initially outnumbered, Napoleon believed he had finally caught the Russians at Eylau thanks to the arrival of flanking corps whose strength, he believed, would decide the battle. However, Russian steadfastness, the effective use of massed artillery, and the lucky appearance of L'Estocq stalled his efforts. Although pushed back, Bennigsen's army remained in good order. This was the first major battle fought by Napoleon that did not result in the routing of the enemy army.

RELATED TOPICS
See also
LOUIS DAVOUT
page 114

MICHEL NEY
page 124

3-SECOND BIOGRAPHIES
ANTON VON L'ESTOCQ
1738–1815
A veteran of the Seven Years' War, L'Estocq was the commander of the only Prussian troops to remain in action in the wake of the disastrous campaign of 1806

LEVIN BENNIGSEN
1745–1826
A German officer in Russian service, Bennigsen had distinguished himself in successive campaigns against the Turks, Poles and Persians and had been the ringleader in the overthrow of Tsar Paul I in 1800

30-SECOND TEXT
Frederick C. Schneid

Fought in the depths of winter, Eylau was at best a marginal victory that cost Napoleon heavy casualties.

FRIEDLAND

the 30-second history

Napoleon decisively defeated the Russian army under Bennigsen at Friedland (14 June 1807). Following the bloody Battle of Eylau in February, the respective armies entered winter quarters in order to rest and reinforce, only resuming the campaign in May. Napoleon found Bennigsen at Friedland and told his retinue, 'The enemy wishes to give battle today; so much the better, it is the anniversary of Marengo.' The battle reflected Napoleon's willingness to attack his enemy at unfavourable odds, knowing his subordinates would 'march to the sound of the guns': the battle began with 40,000 French to 46,000 Russians, but by the end of the day Napoleon had 80,000 on the field against Bennigsen's 60,000. Bennigsen chose his position poorly. The River Alle was at his back, while a more minor watercourse separated the Russian left flank from the rest of the army. Napoleon spotted this defect in deployment, and at five o'clock, no longer outnumbered, he launched a full assault on the Russian left. Within three hours Bennigsen's army was in retreat: with many caught between the French and the river, perhaps 40 per cent of his men were killed, wounded or captured. On 25 June 1807 Tsar Alexander I and Napoleon met at Tilsit, effectively ending the war.

3-SECOND SHOT
Napoleon's victory over the Russians at Friedland concluded the campaign in Poland and resulted in the Peace of Tilsit.

3-MINUTE CODE
After the uncertain outcome of the Battle of Eylau, Napoleon desperately needed a decisive victory to bring Alexander I to heel. However, the Emperor was frustrated by the Russians' determination in battle and escape from numerous *manoeuvres sur les derrières* – all the more so given the supreme over-confidence produced by his previous victory at Austerlitz. Victory at Friedland was therefore particularly sweet, while it also provided the opportunity to make Russia an ally.

RELATED TOPICS
See also
AUSTERLITZ
page 78

EYLAU
page 84

3-SECOND BIOGRAPHY
CLAUDE VICTOR PERRIN
1764–1841
Perrin served as a brigade commander under Napoleon in 1796, division general in 1797, fought at Marengo and Austerlitz. He was promoted to Marshal of France in 1807, for his actions at Friedland

30-SECOND TEXT
Frederick C. Schneid

Translated by Napoleon into the possibility of a long-term alliance with Russia, Friedland offered the Emperor his best chance of defeating Britain.

WAGRAM

the 30-second history

Wagram was the largest battle of
the Napoleonic Wars to date. In April 1809, with
Napoleon focused squarely on Spain, Emperor
Francis I of Austria directed his brother, the
Archduke Charles, to invade Bavaria and expel
the French from Germany. Napoleon, however,
quickly outmanoeuvred Charles and occupied
Vienna. On 21–22 May a massive counter-attack
at Aspern-Essling led to Napoleon's first major
defeat, but the French did not fall back. On the
contrary, the early morning of 5 July saw him
launch a fresh offensive. Fighting continued all
day with heavy losses on both sides. Nevertheless,
the French could not push the Austrians from
their positions. During the night both armies
reorganized and reinforced. The Archduke called
in two outlying corps and directed them against
the French left. When the battle resumed the
next morning, this manoeuvre threatened to
cut Napoleon's communications. In reply, the
Emperor redeployed Masséna's corps and sent in
both the Young Guard and extra artillery. After
desperate fighting the Austrian offensive stalled,
and the tide turned when Davout's corps drove
back the Austrian left compromising Charles'
position. With no hope of reinforcements, the
Austrian commander ordered a withdrawal, while
Francis sued for peace, an armistice signed at
Znaim ending the war three weeks later.

3-SECOND SHOT
The two-day Battle of
Wagram decided the
Austrian war of 1809:
Napoleon almost lost, but
ultimately the French army
managed to outfight the
Archduke Charles.

3-MINUTE CODE
Perhaps the best Allied
general to see action in
the first part of the
Napoleonic Wars, the
Archduke Charles overcame
Napoleon at Aspern-
Essling and almost did so
again at Wagram. Yet
Napoleon had learned from
his previous defeat, and
ensured that he now
enjoyed a substantial
numerical advantage.
The Austrians fought well,
and Charles demonstrated
his martial prowess,
but Napoleon and his
subordinates managed
to deny them victory.

RELATED TOPICS
See also
LOUIS DAVOUT
page 114

ANDRÉ MASSÉNA
page 118

3-SECOND BIOGRAPHIES
ÉTIENNE MACDONALD
1765–1840
An officer of Scottish descent
who distinguished himself at
Wagram and was rewarded
with the rank of marshal

NICOLAS OUDINOT
1767–1842
Commander of II Corps at
Wagram, Oudinot was elevated
to the marshalate for his
services at the battle

ARCHDUKE CHARLES
OF AUSTRIA
1771–1847
A younger brother of Francis I
Charles succeeded in inflicting
a serious defeat on Napoleon
at Aspern-Essling in May 1809

30-SECOND TEXT
Frederick C. Schneid

*Hard-fought and bloody,
Wagram marked the end
of French superiority on
the battlefield.*

DEFEATS

Battle of Bailén Fought on 19 July 1808, the Battle of Bailén saw the surrender of an entire French army to Spanish forces commanded by Francisco-Javier Castaños.

corps The word *corps* (literally 'body') is a short form of *corps d'armée* (roughly 'bodies into which an army is divided'). As for the concept, this was developed by Napoleon in the period 1800–5 as an ideal method of structuring the forces that made up the Grande Armée. Thus, made up of forces of infantry, cavalry and artillery alike, corps were in effect miniature armies that were complete in themselves and could if necessary operate independently.

corps system *see* **corps**. The term 'corps system' is the one generally used to describe this method of articulating large armies.

Grande Armée Literally 'grand army' or 'big army'. Properly speaking, the army commanded by Napoleon himself in the campaigns of 1805–14. However, the term is sometimes used as a synonym for the army of Napoleon as a whole.

le manoeuvre sur les derrières A favourite operational device of Napoleon's, the *manoeuvre sur les derrières* or, in English, 'manoeuvre upon the rear' involved bypassing an enemy army and then swinging round so as to take it from behind.

Ottoman Empire In 1800 the Ottoman (or Turkish) Empire stretched from the frontiers of Hungary and Croatia to the Persian Gulf and the Red Sea. However, constantly troubled by internal revolts, the Turks had great difficulty in maintaining their position in the face of the threat posed by France and Russia.

patriot cause Used in the context of Spain, the term 'patriot cause' refers to the resistance, popular and otherwise, that was put up to Napoleon's attempt from 1808 onwards to transform Spain into a French satellite state.

Peace of Tilsit Signed in July 1807, the Peace of Tilsit saw Napoleon end hostilities with Prussia and Russia in the wake of his crushing victory over the Russians at Friedland. In brief, Prussia was treated with great harshness and stripped of half her territory, but Russia escaped scot-free, Napoleon seeing her as a potential partner in his war with Britain.

Scorched-earth policy The term 'scorched-earth policy' refers to a tactic employed by a retreating army whereby the territory through which it withdraws is reduced to a desert so as to deny its resources to the enemy.

Third Coalition The term 'Third Coalition' refers to the powers that fought Napoleon in 1805, namely Britain, Austria, Russia, Sweden and Naples.

EGYPT

the 30-second history

By 1797 France had triumphed

over the combined efforts of European states but remained at war with Britain. Unable to launch an invasion, the French government instead authorized a descent on Egypt in the mistaken belief that the Ottomans would relinquish it without a fight. Often presented as a daring blow against Britain, instead this was naked imperialism: long since considered a potential colony, Egypt offered a substitute for the possessions of which France was currently being stripped by the British in the West Indies and elsewhere. Given command of the expedition, on 1 July 1798 Napoleon successfully reached Egypt and went on to take Cairo, after a famous victory at the Pyramids. Isolated from France by Nelson's great triumph at the Battle of the Nile, the young general nevertheless tried to modernize Egypt while simultaneously fending off the vengeful Ottomans and indulging in daydreams of marching on India like his hero, Alexander the Great. A pre-emptive invasion of Palestine and Syria shattered one invasion force, while another was destroyed on the Egyptian coast, but, realizing that he could gain no further advantage by remaining in Egypt, Napoleon returned to France in October 1799, an event followed just one month later by the *coup d'état* that brought him to power.

3-SECOND SHOT
Memorable for its ambitious aims and exotic nature, the French invasion of Egypt was the first in a long series of European encounters with the Middle East in modern times.

3-MINUTE CODE
The expedition was a political and military failure. Ultimately, Egypt could never have been held by France (the garrison was forced to surrender by the British in 1801) while its invasion led to revival of the war in Europe and, with this, many French defeats. That said, it shrouded Napoleon with the lustre of the Orient and played an important role in his rise to power.

RELATED TOPICS
See also
FRENCH REVOLUTION
page 22

ELEVATION
page 38

3-SECOND BIOGRAPHIES
MURAD BEY
c. 1750–1801
Along with fellow Mameluke, Ibrahim Bey, joint-ruler of Egypt in 1798, Murad Bey captained Egyptian resistance to French occupation, only to die of bubonic plague in the moment of final victory in 18c

ABD AL-RAHMAN AL-JABART
1753–1825
An Egyptian scholar based in Cairo who had for years been keeping a chronicle of events in the city, al-Jabarti by extension penned what is virtually the only indigenous account of the French occupation of Egypt

30-SECOND TEXT
Alexander Mikaberidze

Despite the military failure, Napoleon's expedition led to the first comprehensive description of Egyptian history and culture.

TRAFALGAR

the 30-second history

Napoleon's military preeminence in Europe was consistently thwarted by the British Royal Navy. However, the latter's greatest victory occurred on 21 October 1805 after Horatio Nelson spotted a Franco-Spanish fleet commanded by Pierre Villeneuve off the coast of Spain. Villeneuve's fleet of 33 ships was larger but could not match its opponents in terms of training and morale. While Villeneuve arranged his fleet in the customary single line, Nelson chose to divide his fleet into two squadrons and drive straight at the enemy – a dangerous manoeuvre since the weak wind could hinder British movement and allow the enemy to pummel the leading ships. However, by piercing Villeneuve's line, Nelson reckoned that he would be able to turn the battle into a series of ship-to-ship duels in which superior British gunnery, seamanship and morale would trump the enemy's numerical superiority. Just before noon, Nelson hoisted the famous signal, 'England expects that every man will do his duty', and commenced the attack. In five hours of fierce fighting, the British completely devastated the enemy, capturing or destroying 22 ships. By contrast, no British vessels were lost, though Nelson himself was mortally wounded by a French sniper.

RELATED TOPIC
See also
AUSTERLITZ
page 78

3-SECOND SHOT
In one of the most decisive naval battles in history, Trafalgar saw a British fleet under Admiral Lord Nelson defeat the Franco-Spanish fleet of Pierre Villeneuve.

3-MINUTE CODE
Coloured though its memory is by patriotic sentiment, Nelson's victory must be taken with a grain of salt. While it removed the immediate threat of a French invasion of Britain, it also demonstrated the inability of a sea power to affect the outcome of a land war, Napoleon going on to defeat the Third Coalition. At the same time, French naval power was not completely destroyed, the ships lost at Trafalgar soon being replaced by new vessels.

3-SECOND BIOGRAPHIE
FEDERICO GRAVINA Y NÁPO
1756–1806
Spain's most distinguished naval officer, Gravina died of wounds sustained at Trafalga

HORATIO NELSON
1758–1806
The greatest commander the Royal Navy has ever produce Nelson played a leading role victories at Cape Saint Vince (1797) and Copenhagen (180 but obtained lasting fame fro his destruction of Napoleon' fleet at the Battle of the Nile

PIERRE DE VILLENEUVE
1763–1806
An aristocrat who served with distinction in the Revolutionary Wars, Villeneu was so distressed by his defe he committed suicide

30-SECOND TEXT
Alexander Mikaberidze

Great victory though it was, Trafalgar had little influence on the course of the war.

DIVISION OF ADMIRAL NELSON

BRITISH FLEET

DIVISION OF VICE-ADMIRAL COLLINGWOOD

CONTINENTAL BLOCKADE

the 30-second history

After his triumphs over Austria, Russia and Prussia, Napoleon again focused on Britain. Unable to attack her directly, he instead instituted a trade embargo whose aim was to weaken Britain economically and destroy her capacity to wage war. Designed to encompass the whole of Europe, this policy is sometimes portrayed as an attempt to protect the latter's nascent industries against British competition. However, in fact the French Empire was rather a captive market in which French goods had free rein. Considered by many scholars to be one of Napoleon's biggest mistakes, the blockade ultimately failed, though it is worth noting that its early years did cause economic hardship for Britain. Still worse, on the continent the result was to dislocate trade, cause the permanent decline of some industries and slow down the progress of others. By 1811, indeed, with British smuggling rife, it was working so badly that Napoleon himself began to abandon it in favour of sanctioning British imports to metropolitan France (only) as a source of much-needed revenue. Yet by then it was too late: large parts of the population had been completely alienated and the French pushed into actions – most notably, intervention in Portugal and the invasion of Russia – that led to strategic disaster.

3-MINUTE CODE
A peculiar aspect of the Continental Blockade was that it did not envisage Britain's complete isolation. Instead, Napoleon wanted to stop the British selling their goods in Europe, while simultaneously allowing them to buy goods from Europe, thereby leading to a massive trade imbalance. Such a goal was by no means unattainable: had he adopted less oppressive tariff policies and harnessed the widespread European resentment of Britain, success might well have been his.

RELATED TOPICS
See also
THE INDUSTRIAL REVOLUTION
page 24

PENINSULAR WAR
page 100

RUSSIA
page 104

30-SECOND TEXT
Alexander Mikaberidze

In the end the Continental Blockade proved a failure, but in its early days it nonetheless almost brought Britain to her knees.

PENINSULAR WAR

the 30-second history

Determined to flex his muscles at every opportunity, in October 1807 Napoleon invaded Portugal. Taking advantage of disputes in the Spanish court, in May 1808 he turned his attention to Spain, ousting the ruling Bourbons in favour of his eldest brother, Joseph. However, this provoked a serious revolt that quickly spread to Portugal. Traditionally, the ensuing war has been seen as a guerrilla struggle, but the reality is very different: the Spaniards and Portuguese alike mostly relied on regular troops, even if many of them at one time or another found themselves operating behind enemy lines. With the Patriot cause under severe pressure in both countries, the French won many victories, but want of resources and the absence of a unified command structure meant that they could never prevail, while resistance to their rule was bolstered by the dispatch of British troops. Had Napoleon taken charge himself, things might have been different, but, aside from one brief visit in the winter of 1808, he delegated command to his marshals. When the French position in Spain was hopelessly destabilized by the invasion of Russia in 1812, led by Wellington, the main Anglo-Portuguese army was able to counter-attack and not just sweep the French across the Pyrenees but also invade France.

RELATED TOPICS
See also
SPAIN
page 68

CONTINENTAL BLOCKADE
page 98

ANDRÉ MASSÉNA
page 118

JEAN-DE-DIEU SOULT
page 126

3-SECOND BIOGRAPHIES
FRANCISCO JAVIER CASTAÑO
1758–1852
Spanish general chiefly known for his triumph in the Battle of Bailén, Castaños co-operated very closely with Wellington in the campaigns of 1811–13

WILLIAM CARR BERESFORD
1768–1856
A British general who was appointed to reorganize the Portuguese army, Beresford gained a narrow victory at Almeida on 16 May 1811

30-SECOND TEXT
Alexander Mikaberidze

The source of many French defeats, the Peninsular War eroded Napoleon's prestige.

5 January 1759
Born in Dublin

1781
Sent to school at Eton

1790
Becomes Member of
Parliament for Trim
in Ireland

1793
After purchasing the rank
of lieutenant colonel,
joins the 33rd Regiment

1799
Joins his brother, Richard,
in India, participates in
the Anglo-Mysore War

1803
Distinguishes himself
during the Anglo-
Maratha War

1806
After returning home,
marries Kitty Pakenham

1808
Defeats the French in
Portugal but is recalled to
face a military inquiry

1809
Returns to the Iberian
Peninsula, where he
conducts masterful
campaigns for the next
five years; is raised to
the peerage as Viscount
Wellington of Talavera

1813
Gains a decisive victory
at Vitoria, expelling the
French from Spain

1814
Returns to England to see
his wife and sons for the
first time in five years
and is received as a hero
by the public. Appointed
ambassador to France

1815
Sent to command Anglo-
Allied army against
Napoleon, who is defeated
at Waterloo; Wellington
becomes Commander-in-
Chief of the Army of
Occupation of France

1818
Survives an assassination
attempt by André
Cantillon, a veteran
of Napoleon's army

1828
Becomes prime minister
of Britain, accepts the
Catholic Emancipation Act

1830
Resigns his post
after making an
uncompromising speech
against political reforms.
In a dramatic loss of
popularity, his London
home, Apsley House, is
stoned by the mob

1834
Declines William IV's
offer of the prime
ministership

14 September 1852
Dies at Walmer Castle;
his funeral procession
to St Paul's Cathedral
attracts over one
million spectators

ARTHUR WELLESLEY,
1st DUKE OF WELLINGTON

Born into an aristocratic Anglo-ish family, Arthur Wellesley enlisted in the British army at an early age and first rose to prominence as the victor of several major battles in India. Having in the process acquired much useful experience, particularly in respect of logistics and alliance diplomacy, in 1805 he returned to Britain, and in 1808 was sent out to the Iberian Peninsula at the head of the British troops dispatched to support the uprising against Napoleon that had broken out in Spain and Portugal. However, an initial victory at Vimeiro followed by controversy over the terms offered to the French garrison of Lisbon, and Wellesley was recalled to London to face a court of inquiry. Exonerated of all wrongdoing, April 1809 he was restored to his command, and thereafter conducted a series of masterful campaigns that demonstrated him to be a brilliant commander who made the best of every situation and possessed enormous strategic insight, as well as a person of the utmost dedication and integrity (between April 1809 and April 1814 he did not take a single day's leave). Ennobled as a viscount 1809 and subsequently elevated to the rank of marquess, earl and finally duke, he won battle after battle and by the end of

1813 had almost entirely driven the French from the Peninsula. Though his masterpiece is often argued to be Salamanca (22 July 1812), his greatest triumph came in 1815 when, supported by the Prussians, he defeated Napoleon at Waterloo, thereby cementing his reputation as one of Britain's greatest military leaders and paving the way for a successful political career in which his most notable achievement was Catholic emancipation.

Notorious for his stern countenance and acerbic temper – he frequently reduced grown men to tears – Wellesley was a man of contrasts: of modest personal tastes yet vigorous sexual appetites; of a keen mind yet intellectual arrogance; of a pronounced sense of duty yet an ability for great injustice and shifting responsibility for mistakes on to others. Along with his aquiline nose, he was instantly recognizable for his peculiar laugh (likened by some wit to a horse with whooping cough!). To later cartoonists, these characteristics made him a figure of fun, but to his soldiers he was 'Old Nosey', a leader notorious for his insistence on the harshest discipline who yet inspired undying trust on account of his unerring ability to win battles without excessive cost to their lives.

Alexander Mikaberidze

RUSSIA

the 30-second history

In 1807 France and Russia forged
a potential alliance via the Peace of Tilsit, but
by 1812 conflicting ambitions had completely
undermined this arrangement. Against the
advice of his associates, in June Napoleon
therefore invaded Russia at the head of 500,000
men. His plan of forcing a quick battle, however,
was foiled, the Russian armies retreating ever
deeper into the interior and carrying out a
scorched-earth policy. Compelled to follow them,
Napoleon's army was decimated by heat, disease
and exhaustion, the result being that when the
Russians finally turned at bay at Borodino,
they held Napoleon to a draw in one of the
bloodiest battles of the century. Pursuing
them to Moscow, the Emperor found the city
abandoned, while it that same night fell prey
to a terrible fire. Some 2,414 kilometres (1,500
miles) from Paris, with insufficient provisions
and winter approaching, Napoleon spent one
month amidst the city ruins before deciding to
turn back. Begun on 19 October, the retreat
was a disaster. Lumbering through the Russian
countryside, the French came under repeated
attack, and were ultimately all but wiped out
at the Berezina River. Delegating command to
a marshal, Napoleon rushed back to Paris where
he was soon organizing a new army.

3-SECOND SHOT
A military catastrophe
memorable for its vast
scope and human tragedy,
the Russian campaign of
1812 shattered Napoleon's
military might and revealed
that, as he himself noted,
'from the sublime to the
ridiculous there is but
one step'.

3-MINUTE CODE
Napoleon always claimed
that it was 'General
Winter' who defeated him
in Russia, but such claims
are at best dubious. The
French army lost half of its
strength in just the first
eight weeks of the war,
while contemporary
meteorological data reveal
that until late November
the winter was unusually
mild. In mid-December
severe frost did set in,
killing off many of the
surviving troops, but by
then the war was lost.

RELATED TOPICS
See also
CONTINENTAL BLOCKADE
page 98

LOUIS DAVOUT
page 114

3-SECOND BIOGRAPHIES
FYODOR ROSTOPCHIN
1763–1826
Governor of Moscow in 1812,
Rostopchin made use of every
means available to rouse the
population against the French
and was partly responsible for
the burning of the city in
September 1812

ALEXANDER I OF RUSSIA
1771–1825
Initially prepared to work with
Napoleon, Alexander I was
driven to break with him in the
wake of the Peace of Tilsit, and
by 1812 had become resolved
on the French ruler's overthrow

30-SECOND TEXT
Alexander Mikaberidze

*Defeat in Russia
was not the end of
Napoleon: it neither
sparked off rebellion
nor smashed his ability
to raise fresh armies.*

LEIPZIG

the 30-second history

Napoleon's defeat in Russia in

1812 triggered resistance across Europe: by the autumn of 1813 the French were fighting not just Britain and Russia, but also Prussia, Sweden and Austria. Determined to retain as much of his empire as he could, Napoleon refused to pull back to the Rhine and the Pyrenees. In Spain this policy led to a heavy defeat at Vitoria, but in Germany the effects were even more serious. After much complex manoeuvring, Napoleon was eventually all but surrounded at Leipzig. Fighting began on 16 October. Heavily outnumbered, the French beat off their opponents and could have got away that night, but Napoleon elected to hang on hoping for a great victory. On 18 October, then, the battle was resumed. The fighting was desperate and bloody as some 380,000 Allied troops attacked 220,000 Frenchmen. Disputing every inch of the ground, the French were still steadily pushed back, while many of their German auxiliaries changed sides. With the battle clearly lost, Napoleon at last ordered a retreat, but there was only one road to safety and this was blocked when a crucial bridge was blown as French troops were crossing it. The result was complete disaster, barely 50,000 men surviving to cross the Rhine to safety.

RELATED TOPICS
See also
RUSSIA
page 104

WATERLOO
page 108

3-SECOND SHOT
The largest battle in European history before the First World War, the Battle of Leipzig shattered Napoleon's control of central Europe and led to the downfall of the French Empire.

3-MINUTE CODE
Known afterwards as the 'Battle of the Nations', Leipzig led to the overthrow of French control in Holland and all the German states and extinguished the last flickering possibility of Napoleon emerging victorious. Yet it did not end the war: repeatedly rejecting terms that would had have kept him on the throne, Napoleon fought to the end and did not surrender until he was defeated by the Allied powers and forced to resign in April 1814.

3-SECOND BIOGRAPHIES
JOZEF PONIATOWSKI
1763–1813
A leading Polish general, Poniatowski was made a marshal on the eve of Leipzig, but was drowned in the course of the retreat

JEAN-BAPTISTE BERNADOTTE
1763–1844
Once one of Napoleon's marshals, by 1813 Bernadotte had become Crown-Prince of Sweden, in which capacity he led the Swedish troops who fought at Leipzig

30-SECOND TEXT
Alexander Mikaberidze

Today the site of the battle is marked with a massive, 100-metre (328-ft) tall monument that was built for the anniversary of the battle in 1913.

WATERLOO

the 30-second history

On 18 June 1815, some 190,000 men converged on a small area of Belgian countryside just south of Brussels. The fate of the entire European continent was at stake. The French launched repeated assaults to break the line of the Anglo-Allied army commanded by the Duke of Wellington. However, thanks to steely resolve and massive firepower, the British and their German, Dutch and Belgian allies held their ground. From late afternoon onwards, some 50,000 Prussians led by Gebhard von Blücher reached the battlefield, shattering the French right flank. Desperate to restore his fortunes, Napoleon sent his elite Imperial Guard in a last-ditch attempt to turn the tide, but even his famed guardsmen could not break through, the result being a general panic that soon had his entire army fleeing the field. Remarkable for its appalling casualties – some 65,000 men (two-thirds of them Frenchmen) – the battle marked the end point of what some contemporaries called the 'Great War', and heralded an era of relative peace in Europe that would last for four decades, while, in testimony to the manner in which Napoleon won the war for posterity, it is a unique event: mention it and most people associate it with the loser (Napoleon) rather than victor (Wellington or Blücher).

3-SECOND SHOT
An iconic battle, Waterloo brought an end to a generation of warfare and provided a lasting metaphor for defeat.

3-MINUTE CODE
Imagining parallel histories is dangerous ground, but one cannot but wonder whether Europe would have been better off had the Napoleonic Wars ended with a French victory. The empire undoubtedly witnessed systematic exploitation and repression, but the French armies also brought with them important reforms built upon the ideals of the French Revolution. That said, as 1815 did not see a wholesale return to 1789, the jury must remain out on this question.

RELATED TOPICS
See also
AUSTERLITZ
page 78

ARTHUR WELLESLEY, 1ST
DUKE OF WELLINGTON
page 102

MICHEL NEY
page 124

3-SECOND BIOGRAPHIES
GEBHARD VON BLÜCHER
1742–1819
A Prussian general who had been one of the few commanders to distinguish himself in 1806, Blücher was a prominent figure in all the campaigns of the years 1813–

HENRY WILLIAM PAGET,
EARL OF UXBRIDGE
1768–1854
Wellington's second in command Uxbridge led a spectacular cavalry charge that bought vital time

30-SECOND TEXT
Alexander Mikaberidze

Discussion of the Batt of Waterloo still rages was it really a German victory rather than a British one?

MARSHALS

MARSHALS
GLOSSARY

Bourbons The French royal family at the time of the French Revolution. Other branches of the family occupied the thrones of Spain and Naples.

corps The words *corps* (literally 'body'') is a short form of *corps d'armée* (roughly 'bodies into which an army is divided'). As for the concept, this was developed by Napoleon in the period 1800–5 as an ideal method of structuring the forces that made up the Grande Armée. Thus, made up of forces of infantry, cavalry and artillery alike, corps were in effect miniature armies that were complete in themselves and could if necessary operate independently.

corps system see **corps**. The term 'corps system' is the one generally used to describe this method of articulating large armies.

The Hundred Days The Hundred Days is the term generally given to the brief period in 1815 when Napoleon resumed power in France following his escape from Elba.

Hussars A form of cavalry much noted for their flamboyant uniforms that appeared in most armies of the Napoleonic period.

le manoeuvre sur les derrières A favourite operational device of Napoleon's, the *manoeuvre sur les derrières* or, in English, 'manoeuvre upon the rear' involved bypassing an enemy army and then swinging round so as to take it from behind.

Marshalate The collective name given to the 26 senior commanders whom Napoleon eventually promoted to the new rank of 'marshal of the empire'. Their badge of office was a ceremonial baton, the fact that many of the men concerned began their career in the rank and file therefore giving rise to the claim that every French soldier had a marshal's baton in his knapsack.

Old Guard A conglomerate of units that was the senior element of Napoleon's Imperial Guard and included several units of infantry and cavalry. Of these, by far the most famous was the Grenadiers à Pied de la Garde Imperiale.

ɪndémiaire uprising A revolt in Paris in
ːtober 1795, the Vendémiaire uprising
ːtapulted Napoleon to prominence on
count of the part that he played in
overthrow.

ɑr of the Third Coalition The War of
ɪ Third Coalition is the name given to
ɪe campaign in the autumn and early
nter of 1805 that saw the battles of
ɑfalgar, Ulm and Austerlitz.

ɪung Guard The most junior element
Napoleon's Imperial Guard and a late
dition to its forces, the Young Guard saw
ɪch action in the campaigns of 1813–14
d was all but completely destroyed at
ɪe Battle of Waterloo.

LOUIS DAVOUT

the 30-second history

3-SECOND SHOT
Napoleon's most capable
marshal and a professional
soldier par excellence,
Davout was nicknamed
'the Terrible' and routinely
received the assignments
that his master considered
crucial to his success.

3-MINUTE CODE
From 1808 onward, the
inability of the marshalate
to succeed at independent
command robbed
Napoleon of the success
that he himself won on the
battlefield. Along with
Masséna and Suchet,
Davout was the exception
to this rule. His ambition,
courage, determination,
sense of duty and absolute
loyalty elevated Davout far
above his contemporaries,
who viewed him with envy
and distaste. Served by
excellent command and
organizational skills,
Davout was the
quintessential marshal
of the First Empire.

Born in 1770, Davout was
commissioned in the French cavalry in 1788, but
supported the Revolution. A veteran of the
campaigns on the Rhine and in Egypt, he was
promoted to general of division in 1800, and in
1804 became the youngest of the 18 original
marshals created by Napoleon. Commanding III
Corps, Davout played a key role in French victories
at Austerlitz (1805), Auerstädt (1806) and Eckmühl
(1809). During the 1812 invasion of Russia, he
commanded the 70,000-man I Corps, defeating
the Russians at Mohilev, participating in the
victory at Borodino, and commanding the
rearguard during the retreat from Moscow
until being replaced by Marshal Ney. Having
successfully defended Hamburg, which Napoleon
considered the key to his German possessions,
during the campaigns of 1813–14, he served the
Emperor as Minister of War during the Hundred
Days and so did not participate in the Waterloo
campaign. Stripped of his honours after
Napoleon's second abdication, he eventually
had his rank and titles restored in 1817. Davout
was a stern disciplinarian who demanded total
obedience from his soldiers and officers but
always strove to keep his men fed and paid.
Unlike many of his fellow marshals, he was
capable of effective independent command and
was both respected and feared by his adversaries.

RELATED TOPICS
See also
JENA-AUERSTÄDT
page 82

EYLAU
page 84

RUSSIA
page 104

3-SECOND BIOGRAPHIE
CHARLES GUDIN DE LA
SABLONNIÈRE
1768–1812
A divisional commander in
Davout's corps who particula
distinguished himself at
Auerstädt, Gudin perished
in the Russian campaign

LOUIS SUCHET
1770–1826
Considered one of Napoleor
most brilliant generals, Such
was made a marshal in 1811
following his successful sieg
of Tarragona

30-SECOND TEXT
Michael Leggiere

*Known as the Iron
Marshal, Davout was a
disciplinarian but also a
mentor to many officers*

MARÉCHAL DAVOUT.

PRINCE D'ECKMÜHL

JEAN LANNES

the 30-second history

Born on 10 April 1769 to a Gascon

peasant and barely educated, Lannes joined the French army on 20 June 1792 and served in the Pyrenees theatre until 1795, attaining the rank of colonel by the end of 1793. He next saw action in Italy in 1796, where he won Napoleon's friendship by leading a counter-attack that prevented his capture at the Battle of Arcola. Thrice-wounded and promoted to general of brigade, in 1798 Lannes was in consequence included in Napoleon's Egyptian campaign, in which he played a key role in the storming of Jaffa. Returning to France with Napoleon, he commanded the French vanguard during the Marengo campaign, served as French ambassador to Portugal in 1801, was named to the marshalate in 1804 and received command of V Corps during the 1805 War of the Third Coalition. Having distinguished himself in this capacity at Ulm, Austerlitz, Jena and Friedland, in November 1808 he accompanied Napoleon to Spain and defeated the Spaniards at Tudela before going on to take Zaragoza in the face of desperate resistance in February 1809. Recalled to take part in the war against Austria, he again commanded Napoleon's vanguard, only to fall mortally wounded at the Battle of Aspern-Essling on 21 May.

RELATED TOPICS
See also
ITALIAN CAMPAIGN
page 74

MARENGO
page 76

AUSTERLITZ
page 78

JENA-AUERSTÄDT
page 82

FRIEDLAND
page 86

3-SECOND SHOT
One of Napoleon's most intrepid marshals and, as such, one who regularly received the most difficult assignments, Lannes was the first marshal to die from battle-inflicted wounds.

3-MINUTE CODE
Although Lannes mostly fought under Napoleon's supervision, he often performed the bloody task of pinning and weakening the enemy through long hours of brutal fighting against almost insurmountable odds to allow the final French blow to be the *coup de grâce*. As Napoleon entrusted this necessary aspect of his campaigning only to his most battle-hardened, courageous and unflappable generals, Lannes would be sorely missed during the campaigns of 1809–14.

30-SECOND TEXT
Michael Leggiere

A great battlefield commander, Lannes was one of Napoleon's few close friends.

ANDRÉ MASSÉNA

the 30-second history

Born in 1758 in the Piedmontese city of Nice to a shopkeeper, Masséna enlisted in the French army as a private in 1775, reaching sergeant-major in 1784. Leaving the army in 1789, he rejoined in 1791 and by 1793 was a general of division. From early 1794 employed in the Army of Italy, he demonstrated outstanding command skills during Napoleon's first Italian Campaign and in 1799 held Switzerland against successive invading Austrian and Russian armies. Just as impressive, meanwhile, was his defence of Genoa in a 60-day siege the following year. Among the 18 generals elevated to the rank of Marshal of the Empire in 1804, in 1805 as commander of the Army of Italy he pinned down the bulk of the Austrian forces, thereby allowing Napoleon to win the great victories of Ulm and Austerlitz. In 1807 Masséna commanded V Corps in Poland, while 1809 saw him lead IV Corps to further glory at the battles of Aspern-Essling and Wagram. During the Peninsular War, Masséna commanded the French Army of Portugal in 1810–11, but, after failing to capture Lisbon, he withdrew to the Spanish frontier and was defeated by Wellington at Fuentes de Oñoro. Recalled to France in disgrace, he never served in the field again, and played no role in the Hundred Days.

3-SECOND SHOT
Napoleon's most experienced marshal, Masséna achieved prominence despite his common origins and lack of a formal military education, and was referred to by Napoleon as 'the greatest name of my military empire'.

3-MINUTE CODE
In his prime, Masséna was a model for many French commanders: so successful was he, in fact, that Napoleon called him 'the dear child of victory'. However, although he understood the Emperor's method of warfare, he was always unpopular with his fellow marshals, while from Genoa onwards he was in poor health. Despite serving gloriously at Aspern-Essling, he was no longer fit for independent command and his stellar record was marred in Portugal and Spain.

RELATED TOPICS
See also
ITALIAN CAMPAIGN
page 74

MARENGO
page 76

WAGRAM
page 88

PENINSULAR WAR
page 100

3-SECOND BIOGRAPHY
JEAN REYNIER
1771–1814
A divisional commander in Masséna's Army of Italy, Reynier led the French invasi of Naples in 1806 and went on to serve under Masséna in Austria in 1809 and Portugal in 1810. Captured at Leipzig, subsequently died of typhus

30-SECOND TEXT
Michael Leggiere

Possibly the greatest of the marshals, on a personal level Massé was an unpleasant character who was much hated.

JOACHIM MURAT

the 30-second history

An innkeeper's son, Murat

enlisted in a light-cavalry regiment in 1787. He was commissioned in 1792 but saw little action until 1795 when he secured Napoleon's patronage by his quick thinking during the Vendémiaire uprising. Appointed to the staff of the Army of Italy, he led his first cavalry charge at the Battle of Dego and was subsequently promoted general of brigade. During the Egyptian campaign, Murat fought in most of the major battles, notably crushing the Turkish flank at Aboukir and earning a promotion to general of division. Back in France, he played a pivotal role in Napoleon's November 1799 coup and then married the new French ruler's 17-year-old sister, Caroline. Second on the list of the newly created marshalate in 1804, Murat performed his greatest service in 1805–7 as commander of Napoleon's Cavalry Reserve by either facilitating the army's great flanking operations (Ulm and Jena), delivering the *coup de grâce* (Austerlitz and Jena) or saving the infantry (Eylau). In 1808 he served as the Lieutenant of the Emperor in Spain and received the crown of Naples that same year. He played key roles in the campaigns of 1812 and 1813 before joining the Allies in a bid to keep his crown. Switching sides again in 1815, Murat was defeated by the Austrians and subsequently executed.

RELATED TOPICS
See also
SPAIN
page 68

ITALIAN CAMPAIGN
page 74

JENA-AUERSTÄDT
page 82

PENINSULAR WAR
page 100

LEIPZIG
page 106

3-SECOND SHOT
One of the very best cavalry commanders in the history of warfare, no other Napoleonic commander did as much to secure Napoleon's greatest victories as Murat.

3-MINUTE CODE
Like Lannes and Ney, Murat was a powerful sword in Napoleon's hands. Although the quintessential cavalry commander of his age if not all of history, he lacked the full understanding of how to integrate all three branches in battle and gave more thought to designing his flamboyant uniforms than to strategic planning. Napoleon valued his leadership, combat skills and élan but detested his womanizing and political ambition.

3-SECOND BIOGRAPHY
CAROLINE BONAPARTE
1782–1839
A younger sister of Napoleon of France, Caroline was a woman of great beauty and is particularly remembered for her hatred of the Empress Josephine

30-SECOND TEXT
Michael Leggiere

One of two of the marshals to die before a firing squad, Murat ended his life as a champion of Italian nationalism.

20 November 1753
Born at Versailles

1766
Joins Engineers

1770
Commissioned as lieutenant of infantry

1776
Transferred to cavalry, rising a year later to the rank of captain

1780
Promoted to captain of infantry; arrives in America, part of French expeditionary force

1783
Returns to France

1787
Joins General Staff Corps, promoted to major a year later

1789
Promoted to lieutenant-colonel; temporary commander of the Versailles National Guard

1792
General officer (*Maréchal de camp*); serves as Chief of Staff to the Armies of the North, Centre and the Rhine; suspended for *incivisme*

1795
Reinstated as general of brigade, named Chief of Staff Army of the Alps; promoted to general of division

1796
Named Chief of Staff Army of Italy; participates in First Italian Campaign

1798
Occupies Rome and creates Roman Republic; recalled to Paris and named Chief of Staff Army of the Orient; participates in Egyptian Campaign

1799
Named Minister of War (until April 1800)

1800
Named Commander in Chief Army of the Reserve; Second Italian Campaign; wounded at Marengo; named Minister of War (until 1807)

1804
Named Marshal of the Empire, first in seniority

1805
Named Chief of Staff of the Grande Armée

1806
Made Prince of Neuchâtel and Valangin

1809
Participates in War of the Fifth Coalition

1812
Participates in Russian campaign

1813
Participates in War of the Sixth Coalition

1814
Made Peer of France by Louis XVIII

1 June 1815
Dies in Bamberg in mysterious circumstance

ALEXANDRE BERTHIER

The oldest son of an engineer lieutenant-colonel, Berthier was born at Versailles on 20 November 1753. Commissioned in 1770, he participated in the American Revolutionary War as an infantry captain but saw little action. Returning to France in 1783, he joined the recently formed general staff and became involved in projects for military reform. Rallying to the Revolution in 1789, he served with the Armies of the North, the Centre and the Rhine, only to be accused of being a royalist and suspended. Recalled to active duty in 1795, he served as Chief of Staff in, first, the Army of the Alps and then the Army of Italy, in which last capacity he inaugurated a partnership with Napoleon that lasted until 1814. Although he took no active part in the coup that brought the latter to power, Berthier was at Napoleon's side as his chief of staff in every campaign that he waged until 1814, and was rewarded with several titles, including Prince of Neuchâtel and Valangin (1806), and Prince of Wagram (1809). That said, he did not rally to Napoleon during the Hundred Days. Opting for exile in Bamberg, Berthier died on 1 June 1815 after falling out of an upstairs window (some accounts claim he was assassinated and others that he jumped to his death out of grief for not answering Napoleon's call).

Although not a field commander, Berthier was by far the most indispensable of the marshals due to his innate understanding of Napoleon's instructions and his ability to issue them as clear, precise directives. With unsurpassed organizational skills, Berthier developed the staff of the Grande Armée into the central nervous system of Napoleon's military machine. Like Napoleon, he could work long hours, sometimes even days, without sleep.

Resembling a grocer more than a general, the short, stocky, good-humoured Berthier insisted on strict procedure and treated his staff firmly but fairly. He could rally troops when necessary as at Lodi, lead a cavalry charge as at Rivoli, and write blistering missives to his fellow marshals when needed. Although Berthier forever stood in Napoleon's shadow, many of the latter's greatest accomplishments would not have been possible without him. As Napoleon lamented after Waterloo, 'Had Berthier been there, I would not have met this misfortune.'

Michael Leggiere

MICHEL NEY

the 30-second history

Born on 10 January 1769, Ney

enlisted in the hussars in 1789. He reached general of division by 1799 and was made a marshal in 1804. At Napoleon's side during all the major campaigns and battles of the imperial era, and an intrepid soldier as well as a first-rate administrator and disciplinarian, Ney flourished as a tactician and commanded VI Corps of the Grande Armée at Ulm, Jena, Eylau and Friedland. Sent to help restore order in Spain and Portugal in 1808, he fought in Galicia in 1809 and Portugal in 1810–11, but sharp differences with Masséna led to him being sent back to France in disgrace. Subsequently rehabilitated, he led III Corps with great distinction at Borodino before commanding the rearguard in the retreat from Moscow. In spring 1813 he again commanded III Corps, bearing the brunt of the Allied attack at Lützen but missing an opportunity to encircle the Allied army at Bautzen. Defeated at Dennewitz at the head of the Army of Berlin in 1813, in 1814 he saw action in several battles in the defence of France before leading the coup that forced Napoleon's abdication. Despite serving Louis XVIII, Ney joined Napoleon during the Hundred Days, a decision which led him to being tried for treason and executed by firing squad.

RELATED TOPICS
See also
RUSSIA
page 104

WATERLOO
page 108

ANDRÉ MASSÉNA
page 118

3-SECOND BIOGRAPHY
LOUIS XVIII
1755–1824
King of France from 1814 to 1824, Louis was placed on the throne by the victorious Allied powers and wanted to rule as moderate but faced mounting pressure from ultra-royalists who wanted to reverse the accomplishments of the French Revolution

30-SECOND TEXT
Michael Leggiere

3-SECOND SHOT
Nicknamed 'the bravest of the brave' by Napoleon, Ney saw more action in the French wars than any other French marshal.

3-MINUTE CODE
Although a powerful sword in his emperor's hand, Ney was ill-suited to independent command and often lost sight of the big picture during the heat of battle: at Waterloo, for example, it was he who launched the ill-conceived cavalry attacks that bled the French dry and he again who was responsible for the famous attack of the Guard being so bungled. Temperamental, confrontational and uncooperative, he also disliked Napoleon on a personal level.

Often blamed for defeat at Waterloo, Ney ought rather to be remembered for his extraordinary feats of leadership in the retreat from Moscow.

JEAN-DE-DIEU SOULT

the 30-second history

3-SECOND SHOT
One of Napoleon's most trusted subordinates, Soult was nicknamed the 'Hand of Iron' by his men. However, while an excellent organizer and strategist, in battle he was less adept.

3-MINUTE CODE
Evaluating Soult is difficult. Unlike the majority of the marshals, he appears to have had a good grasp of Napoleon's operational and strategic methods, and yet he often failed on the battlefield while at the same time never quite living up to the promise he displayed in his younger years. Though held in high esteem by Napoleon, he could not control his ambition and was hated by most of his subordinates and fellow commanders.

After enlisting in 1785 at the age of 16 and being commissioned in 1792, Soult earned a reputation for leading from the front. Promoted to general of brigade in 1794, by 1799 he had risen to general of division and in this capacity assisted Masséna in his defence of Switzerland. Captured after suffering a leg-shattering wound during one of the many sorties he led during the siege of Genoa in 1800, he emerged from the campaign with a permanent limp, and he was thereafter much more timorous and concerned for his own safety. Nevertheless, Soult became a marshal in 1804 and commanded IV Corps during the Ulm, Austerlitz, Jena and Eylau campaigns. Accompanying Napoleon to Spain in November 1808, he remained there for most of the next five years, accumulating a mixed record. After temporarily serving in the German theatre in 1813, he returned to what was now the Pyrenean front in the wake of the decisive French defeat at Vitoria, and spent the rest of the war first trying to force Wellington's army back from the French frontier and then conducting the defence of southwest France. Minister of War under Louis XVIII, he nevertheless declared for Napoleon during the Hundred Days, and was appointed chief of staff.

RELATED TOPICS
See also
SPAIN
page 68

AUSTERLITZ
page 78

JENA–AUERSTÄDT
page 82

PENINSULAR WAR
page 100

WATERLOO
page 108

3-SECOND BIOGRAPHY
ALFRED DE SAINT-CHAMAN
1781–1848
A cavalry officer of noble origins who enlisted in the army in 1801 who was appointed to Soult's staff in 1809, Saint-Chamans quickly developed a deep loathing for his commander and went on to paint a very hostile picture of him in his memoirs

30-SECOND TEXT
Michael Leggiere

Appointed chief of staff in 1815, Soult proved a poor substitute for Marshal Berthier.

MARÉCHAL-GÉNÉRAL SOU
DUC DE DALMATIE

Schloditten

Pr EYLAU

BATAILLE DE TOULOUS

CLAUDE VICTOR PERRIN

the 30-second history

Born at Lamarche in 1764, Perrin

enlisted in the French army in 1781. Following a brief return to civilian life, in 1792 he re-enlisted and by 1793 he was a lieutenant-colonel in which capacity he earned the esteem of Napoleon during the capture of Toulon. Rewarded with Napoleon's patronage, he served under him in his two Italian campaigns, but, despite his solid performance, was not made a marshal in 1804 due to his republican sympathies. Now operating under the pseudonym of Victor (his middle name), he distinguished himself at Friedland and got his marshal's baton one month later. In the autumn of 1808 Victor went to Spain and gained a victory at Gamonal, but was defeated by Wellington at Talavera and frustrated in an attempt to capture Cádiz, later suffering a further defeat at Barrosa. Recalled to command IX Corps during the Russian campaign, Victor performed his main service by protecting the army as it retreated across the Berezina river. Assuming command of II Corps, he fought at both Dresden and Leipzig, and saw much action in 1814 until he was relieved of his command by the Emperor for arriving late at the Battle of Montereau. During the Hundred Days, Victor remained loyal to Louis XVIII, and later voted for the execution of Ney.

RELATED TOPICS
See also
ITALIAN CAMPAIGN
page 74

MARENGO
page 76

FRIEDLAND
page 86

PENINSULAR WAR
page 100

LEIPZIG
page 106

3-SECOND SHOT
Added to the marshalate in 1807, Claude Victor Perrin, who epitomized the French saying that every soldier carried a marshal's baton in his knapsack, displayed organizational and tactical skills, but was an overly cautious strategist.

3-MINUTE CODE
Not Napoleon's finest marshal, Victor was something of an enigma both as a general and a person. His positive attributes included bravery, *sang-froid* and tenacity, but he was a clumsy tactician, a poor subordinate to all but Napoleon and lax in his conduct of operations. He related to his men well, but, except for Lannes, had no friends among his fellow marshals, and became increasingly embittered by what he perceived as a series of slights.

30-SECOND TEXT
Michael Leggiere

A tough and forceful commander, Victor lacked subtlety on the battlefield.

VICTOR.

TOOLS ◐

anti-clericalism A term used to describe hostility to the Catholic Church. At the level of the streets exemplified by mockery of the clergy and, on occasion, violence; at the level of rulers and governments, it found expression in attempts to reduce the power of the papacy, to subject the Church to greater state control and to abolish the religious orders.

column, line, square The words 'column', 'line' and 'square' are used to describe formations used on the battlefield by Napoleon's army and its opponents, all of them being particularly associated with the infantry.

corps system The words *corps* (literally 'body') is a short form of *corps d'armée* (roughly 'bodies into which an army is divided'). As for the concept, this was developed by Napoleon in the period 1800–5 as an ideal method of structuring the forces that made up the Grande Armée. Thus, made up of forces of infantry, cavalry and artillery alike, corps were in effect miniature armies that were complete in themselves and could if necessary operate independently. The term 'corps system' is the one generally used to describe this method of articulating large armies.

Coup of 18 Brumaire A date in the new calendar adopted by the newly formed French Republic in 1792 that corresponds to 9 November, 18 Brumaire was the day in 1799 when a Napoleon freshly returned from Egypt seized power in Paris with the help of the army.

Girondins The Girondins were a Revolutionary faction who took the lead in precipitating the War of the First Coalition and establishing the Republic in 1792. Also known as the Brissotins, they were overthrown the following year by the faction headed by Maximilien Robespierre known as the Montagnards.

Grande Armée Literally 'grand army' or 'big army'. Properly speaking, the army commanded by Napoleon himself in the campaigns of 1805–14. However, the term is sometimes used as a synonym for the army of Napoleon as a whole.

i Jourdan A law passed in the French
sembly in September 1798 that
tablished a regular system of
nscription to the French army on
e basis of the principle of universal
litary service.

manoeuvre sur les derrières A favourite
erational device of Napoleon's, the
anoeuvre sur les derrières or, in
glish, 'manoeuvre upon the rear'
volved bypassing an enemy army
d then swinging round so as to take
from behind.

ar of the First Coalition A conflict that
oke out in 1792 and lasted till 1797, the
ar of the First Coalition saw a range of
ropean states take arms against the
nch Revolution, only to be forced,
e by one, to make peace.

ARMY

the 30-second history

Made up of the usual mixture of infantry, cavalry, artillery and service troops such as engineers, the French army was transformed by Napoleon and became the central pillar of his imperial project. However, the changes made under his rule did not concern matters of recruitment, composition, armament, tactics or even basic organization: in all these areas, the army that fought for Napoleon was essentially the same as the army that fought for the French Revolution. For example, the men were conscripts with an admixture of foreign volunteers; the officer corps a mixture of nobles and commoners recruited according to the principle that promotion should be based on merit rather than birth; the weapons the standard sabres, muskets and smooth-bore cannon of the eighteenth century; the tactics a mixture of column, line and square, as appropriate. Napoleon made a difference first, in his introduction of the corps system (in brief, a way of ordering the army's regiments at the highest level that greatly increased its striking power on the battlefield and its flexibility and speed of manoeuvre off it); second, in his success in developing a personal relationship with his soldiers that almost to the very end kept them convinced that their interests and his were identical; and, third, in his encouragement within the army of a spirit of competition.

3-SECOND SHOT
Hard to beat in battle, it was above all the French army that made Napoleon master of Europe.

3-MINUTE CODE
The successes of Napoleon's army caused the other continental powers to develop mass conscript armies of their own, while at the same time encouraging leading military thinkers across Europe to think in terms of decisive battles that, like Austerlitz or Wagram, could end whole campaigns at a stroke. In 1914, this was to lead to disaster.

RELATED TOPICS
See also
CONSCRIPTION
page 144

LEGION OF HONOUR
page 146

3-SECOND BIOGRAPHY
LAZARE, COMTE CARNOT
1753–1823
French politician and engineer whose organizational ability in the creation of the French Revolutionary Army in the 1790s did much to establish it as a formidable force in the following decades

30-SECOND TEXT
Charles J. Esdaile

One of Napoleon's strengths was his ability to inspire his troops at every level, imbuing them with the conviction that they would succeed.

ART

the 30-second history

Keenly aware of the value of propaganda of all types, Napoleon mobilized French artists in support of his regime, offering them massive financial rewards in exchange for depicting him favourably. As a result a series of artists including Antoine Gros, Jacques-Louis David, Jean Ingres and Louis Lejeune produced a large number of works which can be divided into portraits of Napoleon, battle scenes, events in Napoleon's life and allegories of various sorts. In so few words it is difficult even to introduce the subject effectively. Suffice to say that most images of Napoleon current in the modern world are the fruit not of the counter-propaganda of caricaturists such as James Gillray but of these imperial painters. For example, the familiar depiction of Napoleon arrayed in a long greatcoat and a low cocked hat, and almost invariably standing on his own, is a product of the last years of the empire, depicting, as it does, an emperor who is 'every man' as well as one who is standing alone against the world. If images of this sort were manipulated, so were many of the other categories of representation listed here: taking Lejeune's canvas of the Battle of Marengo as an example, this conveys a wildly misleading impression of the climax of the day.

3-SECOND SHOT
Napoleon's greatest contribution to the world of art was not the works he commissioned, but rather his patronage of the Louvre.

3-MINUTE CODE
The most famous single image of Napoleon is probably that painted by David showing him crossing the St Bernard Pass in 1800 astride a splendid charger. This Romantic treatment shows him battling both geography and climate, and identifies him with such qualities as youth, dynamism and hope, while simultaneously reminding the viewer that he was following in the footsteps of Hannibal and Charlemagne (the rocks beside the track are carved with their names).

RELATED TOPICS
See also
JACQUES-LOUIS DAVID
page 138

PRESS
page 148

3-SECOND BIOGRAPHIE
JAMES GILLRAY
1756–1815
English caricaturist who was particularly savage in his excoriation of Napoleon

ANTOINE-JEAN GROS
1771–1835
Disciple of David who becam famous for such works as *Bonaparte au pont d'Arcole*

LOUIS-FRANÇOIS LEJEUNE
1775–1848
French general who produce many battle scenes after 181

JEAN INGRES
1780–1867
French Neo-Classicist painte who studied under David

30-SECOND TEXT
Charles J. Esdaile

The Napoleonic epoch produced many famo paintings, but few great works of art.

30 August 1748
Born in Paris

1766
Enters the Royal Academy
of Painting and Sculpture

1774
Wins the Prix de Rome
and travels to Italy

1780
Returns to Paris

1786–9
Exhibits *The Oath of
the Horatii*

1787
Exhibits *The Death
of Socrates*

1789
Exhibits *The Lictors bring
to Brutus the Bodies of
his Sons*

1789
Commissioned to paint
The Tennis Court Oath

1792
Abandons work on *The
Tennis Court Oath*
following proclamation
of the Republic

1793
Exhibits *The Death of
Marat* and *The Last
Moments of Michel
Lepeletier Assassinated*;
sketches Marie-Antoinette
on her way to execution

1793–4
Acts as the producer of a
series of public festivals
culminating in the
so-called 'Feast of the
Supreme Being'

1794–5
Imprisoned twice in the
wake of the fall of
Robespierre; narrowly
escapes being guillotined

1799
Exhibits *The Intervention
of the Sabine Women*

1801
Exhibits *Napoleon
Crossing the Alps*

1806
Exhibits *The Coronation of
Napoleon in Notre Dame*

1812
Exhibits *The Emperor
Napoleon in his Study in
the Tuileries*

1814
Flees to Brussels

1825
Exhibits *Mars Being
Disarmed by Venus and
the Three Graces*

29 December 1825
Dies in Brussels after
being knocked down by
a carriage

JACQUES-LOUIS DAVID

Born in Paris in 1748, David came from a prosperous family. Originally intended as an architect, he displayed so much talent as an artist that he was instead sent to study painting under the well-known Joseph-Marie Vien, with whose guidance he secured place at the Royal Academy of Painting and Sculpture and went on to win the prestigious Prix de Rome, a generous scholarship that enabled the winner to study in Rome for three years. Returning to Paris much influenced by the Neo-Classicist movement and the writings of Jean-Jacques Rousseau, he became a professor of the Royal Academy himself and was granted a grace and favour apartment in the Louvre in which capacity he painted the great Neo-Classic trilogy constituted by *The Oath of the Horatii*, *The Death of Socrates* and *The Lictors bring to Brutus the Bodies of his Sons*.

The last of these works actually appeared in 1789, at which point the French Revolution intervened. As all three of his trilogy had hinted in various ways, David was very much in sympathy with the ideals of the Revolution: indeed, more than that, he had become a republican. That being the case, he was a natural choice when the radical faction known as the Jacobin Club commissioned him to paint an enormous canvas showing the inaugural act of the Revolution, namely the famous *Tennis Court Oath* of 1789. In the end, the commission had to be abandoned for political reasons – the version that is often reproduced of it is but a sketch – but in 1793 David did complete an overt statement of support for the Revolution in the form of *The Death of Marat*, though much of his time at this period was taken up with acting as the producer of a series of great public festivals (and also, hilariously, with the design of a specifically 'Republican' national costume that sought to do away with knee-breeches and trousers in favour of Roman-style tunics).

Despite his Republican convictions, David had no hesitation in serving Napoleon after 1799, becoming his *de facto* court painter and producing studies of the crossing of the St Bernard Pass, the coronation and Napoleon surrounded by his papers in his private office. Following Napoleon's defeat he fled into exile for fear of persecution and settled in Brussels where he died some 11 years later after being struck by a carriage.

Charles J. Esdaile

THE CIVIL CODE

the 30-second history

The Civil Code, or 'Code Napoleon', was published in March 1804, and was the fruit of the massive homogenization of French law embarked upon in the wake of the French Revolution (hitherto France had been subject to many different codes of law, while the need to take action was reinforced still further by the abolition of the manorial courts, this leaving large parts of France without any law at all). Progress having been very slow, Napoleon took control when he became First Consul, setting up a committee of four senior judges to address the task and frequently chairing discussion himself. Ever since its publication, the resulting document has been hailed for its establishment of a system of justice that was so well organized and accessible that it remains the basis of the French judicial system to this day. As the frontiers of the empire continued to expand, meanwhile, so the reach of the Code expanded with it, Napoleon being very strongly in favour of its imposition throughout the empire, though, in fact, such was the resistance from local élites that this goal was never fully attained.

3-SECOND SHOT
With the pithy comment 'There are so many laws that no-one is safe from hanging' Napoleon summed up the need for a codification of the law when he assumed power in 1799.

3-MINUTE CODE
The Civil Code is often regarded as a charter of liberty. In fact, this was far from true. Women lost a number of rights that they had acquired since 1789, while the head of each household was made legally responsible for the behaviour of his household via the power to incarcerate family members who flouted his authority, thereby making him an agent of the police.

RELATED TOPIC
See also
NEO-CLASSICISM
page 28

3-SECOND BIOGRAPHIES
JEAN RÉGIS DE CAMBACÉRÈS
1753–1824
Minister of Justice in 1799 and chairman of the committee set up to produce the Civil Code, Cambacérès had been a strong advocate of legal reform in the Republic, and was in part appointed Second Consul on account of his expertise

LOUIS FAURE
1760–1837
Respected jurist who became member of the new parliament established in the wake of the overthrow of the regime of Robespierre, Faure was one of the four judges appointed by Napoleon to sit on the committee that produced the Civil Code

30-SECOND TEXT
Charles J. Esdaile

Though often the subject of favourable comment, the Civil Code was in fact one more emanation of the Napoleonic police state.

CODE CIVIL
DES FRANÇAIS.

TITRE PRÉLIMINAIRE.

DE LA PUBLICATION, DES EFFETS
ET DE L'APPLICATION DES LOIS
EN GÉNÉRAL.

ARTICLE I.er

...ois sont exécutoires dans tout le territoire français,
...u de la promulgation qui en est faite par le PREMIER

...ront exécutées dans chaque partie de la Répu-
...ent où la promulgation en pourra être

...PREMIER CONSUL sera répu-
...aura son siège le Gouvernement,
...a promulgation, et dans chacun
...ement, c'est-à-dire à même délai,
...lieue de myria-
...l'on comptera dix où là

THE CONCORDAT

the 30-second history

The French Revolution led to
severe conflict between Church and state.
Convinced that the Catholic Church was
opposed to freedom and an impediment to
economic development, the Revolutionaries
launched a bitter attack upon it that at times
was so savage it amounted to an attempt to
eradicate Christianity altogether. However, this
proved counter-productive: though it would be
wrong to ascribe the massive popular resistance
faced by the Revolution from 1792 onwards
entirely to religious issues, the defence of the
Church provided a useful rallying cry for both
Royalist aristocrats and peasant rebels, the
result being that France was convulsed by a
series of rebellions. Eager to put an end to this
situation, Napoleon also saw that there was no
need to abolish the Church, even were such a
policy not completely counter-productive,
believing that it could rather be co-opted and
transformed into an agent of social and political
control. In brief, he therefore offered Pope Pius
VII a deal known as the Concordat whereby
the Church would be allowed to continue to
operate and compensated for loss of its lands
during the Revolution in exchange for giving its
full backing to the regime and allowing
Napoleon to choose its bishops.

RELATED TOPIC
See also
THE ENLIGHTENMENT
page 18

3-SECOND SHOT
In pushing for the
surrender of the Catholic
Church to his demands,
Napoleon (a convinced
agnostic) claimed that he
was the ruler of France
by divine right.

3-MINUTE CODE
Initially, the Concordat
worked well, but
ever-growing pressure
on Napoleon's part led
to ever-greater levels of
clerical resistance while the
Emperor's take-over of
Rome in 1807 led to direct
conflict with Pius VII, who
was eventually arrested
and imprisoned in France.
Meanwhile, still more
problems arose on account
of the refusal of 13
cardinals to recognize
Napoleon's divorce of
Josephine and remarriage
to Marie-Louise.

3-SECOND BIOGRAPHIES
JEAN-BAPTISTE DE BELLOY
1709–1808
Bishop of Marseilles, Belloy s
such example of compliance i
respect of the new regime tha
he was rewarded by Napoleor
with the Archbishopric of Par

ERCO CONSALVI
1757–1824
Pius VII's Secretary of State
from 1800 till 1806, Consalvi
played a key role in the
elaboration of the Concordat
but always remained a fierce
opponent of Napoleon

30-SECOND TEXT
Charles J. Esdaile

*Although the
Concordat ended
religious persecution
in France, it proved
a poor bargain for
the Church.*

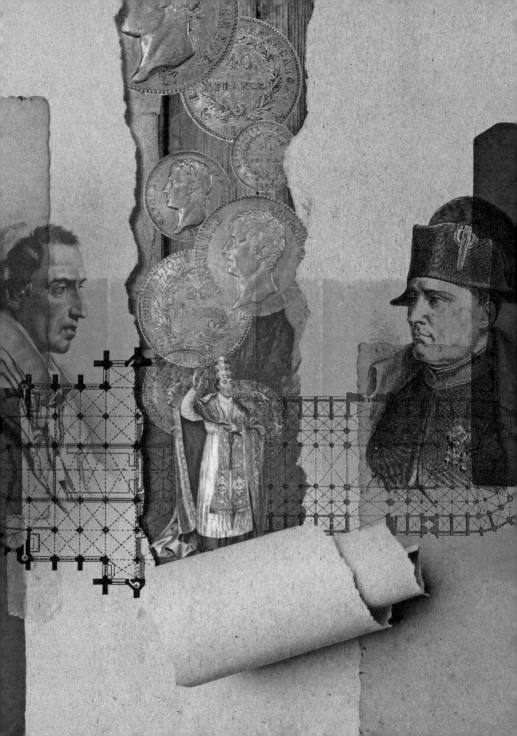

CONSCRIPTION

the 30-second history

With the exception of the assorted deserters and prisoners of war who *chose* to join its various foreign units, the French army Napoleon inherited was entirely recruited by conscription. The basis of the system was the so-called Loi Jourdan of 1798, this making most unmarried males who met certain basic physical standards available for military service when they reached the age of 20 (there were a few exemptions, most of them compassionate). However, service was not universal: each municipality was accorded a certain quota in line with its population, and a public ballot was then held to decide who should actually go. Even then, an unlucky number was not the end of the road: men who had the money could purchase a substitute to take their place, though they might still be called to serve in subsequent levies. As the years passed and the military needs of an empire driven into repeated wars by Napoleon increased, so the number of men required rose dramatically, and the result was that service in the army became ever more likely, not least because the cost of hiring a substitute also soared. In all, some 2,200,000 men were taken of whom as many as 40 per cent never returned.

RELATED TOPIC
See also
ARMY
page 134

3-SECOND SHOT
Given that his army was raised entirely from conscripts, Napoleon's greatest achievement was the extraordinary devotion he was able to command to the very end.

3-MINUTE CODE
From the moment of its introduction, conscription was hated: few young men wanted to leave their families, while the purchase of substitutes was widely regarded as being deeply unjust. Resistance by means of flight, fraud and self-mutilation was common, while many men sought to marry as quickly as possible so as to qualify for exemption. So great was the problem of draft resistance that Napoleon only resolved it by using the harshest of police measures.

3-SECOND BIOGRAPHY
JEAN-BAPTISTE JOURDAN
1762–1833
French general who enlisted as a private in 1778 and rose to the rank of Marshal of the Empire in 1804. By no means a great commander, his name is particularly associated with the conscription law of 1798 because he happened to be president of the chamber of deputies when it was promulgated

30-SECOND TEXT
Charles J. Esdaile

Conscription in France did not originate with Napoleon, but it was under his rule that it became fully effective

LEGION OF HONOUR

the 30-second history

RELATED TOPIC
See also
ARMY
page 134

30-SECOND TEXT
Charles J. Esdaile

Because the Revolution abolished all orders of nobility, when Napoleon became First Consul he sought a new way of rewarding those who had served France (and, by extension, himself) in an exceptional fashion: in his eyes, men acted not out of altruism, but rather needed the stimulus of tangible material rewards. Inaugurated in 1802, his answer was the Legion of Honour, the civil and military order of merit that to this day remains the highest award of the French state. The centrepiece of this was the actual decoration, a white-enamelled medal of an entirely new 'sunburst' design shorn of the Christian symbolism (for example, use of a cross or a star) inherent in the regalia of the old orders of nobility, but recipients (who were divided into five classes) were paid annual pensions ranging from 250 to 5,000 francs. The first distribution of the medal was in a public ceremony held at the Invalides in July 1804. In January 1805 the order was embellished with a new distinction, the *grand aigle*, namely a Napoleonic eagle mounted on a silver star. Portraits of Napoleon, who had no hesitation in making himself a member, almost invariably show him wearing the medal and *grand aigle* alongside one another.

3-SECOND SHOT
The Legion of Honour, an order of merit chiefly distributed to the army, was the product of the notion that, as Napoleon once declared, 'It is by such baubles that men are led.'

3-MINUTE CODE
In theory, the Legion of Honour was open to all French citizens, both soldiers and civilians, but in practice the military dominated its ranks right from the outset: the first recipients included only 12 men who were not soldiers, while by 1814 the award had been made to only 1,500 civilians as opposed to 30,500 soldiers. Under Napoleon, then, merit was military.

The Legion of Honour remains France's most important decoration to this day.

PRESS

the 30-second history

The Revolution led to an

extraordinary explosion in both the extent of the French press and the freedom it enjoyed: 1789 alone saw the appearance of over 130 new newspapers, while during the Revolutionary decade at least 2,000 were published, although many of them only operated for a fairly short time. Debate, meanwhile, was vigorous, and many journalists had no hesitation in lambasting either the government of the day or such targets as individual generals and ministers. As an up-and-coming military commander, Napoleon was well aware of the value of the press and had made good use of it, even founding two newspapers so as to extol his achievements in Italy. By then, however, the Revolutionary journalist's heyday was over: from 1795 onwards, the more conservative regimes that ran France following the fall of Robespierre began to curb press freedom as part of a general push to restore stability to France. Once in power, Napoleon accelerated this process enormously, eventually reducing the number of national newspapers to just four. The Emperor regarding the press as one more weapon of war, he himself wrote many articles for papers such as *Le Moniteur*, and offered substantial rewards to writers willing to pen the sort of material he wanted.

3-SECOND SHOT
Under the empire the press was not free: a system of prior censorship was introduced and editors could be fined or imprisoned if they contradicted the official view.

3-MINUTE CODE
As French rule expanded in areas such as Spain, the first thing the marshals and other commanders did was set up pro-French newspapers. These contained a mixture of articles lifted straight from the Paris press and items contributed by local sympathizers. Also important, meanwhile, was their function as a means of publicizing the decrees of the collaborationist government of King Joseph and the orders of the military authorities.

RELATED TOPIC
See also
ART
page 136

3-SECOND BIOGRAPHY
MARC JULLIEN
1775–1848
Jacobin journalist who accompanied Napoleon to be Italy and Egypt, and played a important role in burnishing the future ruler's reputation this service earning him the Legion of Honour in 1804

30-SECOND TEXT
Charles J. Esdaile

Newspapers played a key role in the Napoleonic system, but freedom of the press was non-exister

Dépêches importantes et officielles envoyées au Gouvernement par M. l'amiral Baudin.

Détails exacts du terrible combat qui a eu lieu sur mer, entre les Français et les Mexicains, où assistait S. A. R. Monseigneur le Prince de Joinville, qui a pris la part la plus honorable au Bombardement et à la Prise de la Vera-Cruz. — Nombre des tués et blessés. — Réddition du Château et du Fort de San-Juan d'Ulloa, 8100 boulets et 320 bombes ont été lancés sur ce Fort. — Courage et intrépidité des Français en cette occasion. — Capitulation signée par M. l'amiral Baudin.

LE MONITEUR

JANVIER 1844

GAZETTE NATIONALE

POÉSIES POLIT

POLITIQUE

MARC-ANTOINE JULLIEN

LE DOUBLE MON

DU 20 JANVIER 1

Paris, ce 24 Thermidor, an second de la
République Française.

MARC-ANTOINE JULLIEN,

Aux Représentans du Peuple composant le
Comité de Salut Public.

MONITEUR

SUPPRIMÉ

BLE MONITEUR

CITOYENS REPRÉSENTANS

1844
595

SIBLINGS

the 30-second history

Napoleon came from a large family, and in all had four brothers and three sisters. Of these, no fewer than four – Joseph, Louis, Jerome and Caroline – became reigning monarchs, while Elise and Pauline were both given Italian duchies, only Lucien being excluded from the general bounty (having played an important role in the Coup of 18 Brumaire, he had then fallen out with Napoleon and retired to private life). The elevation of Napoleon's siblings was not the fruit of generosity, however: rather they were expected to act as the Emperor's agents, integrating their domains into the wider empire, enforcing the Continental Blockade, and raising men and money for his wars (on occasion, too, they were expected to play a role in French marriage diplomacy, Jerome being forced to divorce his first wife and marry a German princess). Such subservience was not to their taste, however, and all the more so as Napoleon bombarded them with frequent sermons as to what they should be doing. To a greater or lesser extent, all of them therefore exhibited a degree of recalcitrance, relations between Louis, who had been made King of Holland, and Napoleon eventually becoming so bad that he was driven from the throne and his realm annexed to France.

RELATED TOPICS
See also
HOLLAND
page 58

GERMANY
page 62

ITALY
page 64

SPAIN
page 68

3-SECOND SHOT
Siblings of the Emperor or not, Napoleon's brothers and sisters were in the end but tools of the imperial will.

3-MINUTE CODE
Pro-Napoleonic historians have often used Napoleon's siblings both as a justification for his conquests and an excuse for his downfall (saying, on the one hand, the Emperor was driven by a desire to advance their status, and, on the other, that he was in every case let down by their incompetence). Such claims are nonsense, however: Napoleon conquered Europe for himself alone, and was overthrown by the faults, not of others, but of himself.

3-SECOND BIOGRAPHIES
JOSEPH BONAPARTE
1768–1844
Napoleon's elder brother, he was elevated to the throne of Naples in 1806 and then transferred to Spain in 1808

LOUIS BONAPARTE
1778–1846
The fourth of the five Bonaparte brothers, Louis was made King of Holland in 1806 but broke with Napoleon in 1809

30-SECOND TEXT
Charles J. Esdaile

Napoleon's siblings were unreliable and quarrelsome, but they played a key role in the French Empire.

APPENDICES

RESOURCES

BOOKS

The Art of War in the Age of Napoleon
Gunther E. Rothenberg
(Indiana University Press, 1978)

Citizen Emperor: Napoleon in Power, 1799–1815
Philip Dwyer
(Bloomsbury, 2013)

Conscripts and Deserters: the Army and French
Society during the Revolution and Empire
Alan Forrest
(Oxford University Press, 1989)

Europe under Napoleon, 1799–1815
Michael Broers
(Arnold, 1996)

Napoleon's Conquest of Europe:
The War of the Third Coalition
Frederick C. Schneid
(Praeger, 2005)

Napoleon's Egypt: Invading the Middle East
Juan Ricardo Cole
(Palgrave Macmillan, 2007)

Napoleon: the End of Glory
Munro Price
(Oxford University Press, 2014)

Napoleon, France and Waterloo:
the Eagle Rejected
Charles J. Esdaile
(Pen & Sword, 2016)

Napoleon as a General: Command
from the Battlefield to Grand Strategy
Jonathan Riley
(Hambledon Continuum, 2007)

Napoleon. Life, Legacy and Image:
A Biography
Alan Forrest
(Quercus, 2011)

Napoleon's Marshals
Edited by David G. Chandler
(Macmillan, 1987)

Napoleon's Men: the Soldiers of
the Revolution and Empire
Alan Forrest
(Hambledon Continuum, 2002).

Napoleon and the Operational Art of War
Edited by Michael V. Leggiere
(Brill, 2016)

Napoleon: the Path to Power, 1769–1799
Phillip Dwyer
(Bloomsbury, 2008)

Napoleon, Soldier of Destiny
Michael Broers
(Faber, 2014)

Napoleon and the Struggle for Germany:
The Franco-Prussian War of 1813
Michael V. Leggiere
(Cambridge University Press, 2015)

Napoleon on War
Bruno Colson
(Oxford University Press, 2015)

Napoleon's Great Escape:
The Battle of the Berezina
Alexander Mikaberidze
(Pen & Sword, 2010)

Napoleon's Trial by Fire:
The Burning of Moscow, 1812
Alexander Mikaberidze
(Pen & Sword, 2014)

Napoleon's Wars: an International History
Charles J. Esdaile
(Allen Lane, 2007)

The Peninsular War: A New History
Charles J. Esdaile
(Allen Lane, 2002)

The Road to Rivoli:
Napoleon's First Campaign
Martin Boycott-Brown
(Cassel, 2001)

Revisiting Napoleon's Continental System:
Local, Regional and European Experiences
Edited by Katherine Aaslestad and Johan Joor
(Palgrave Macmillan, 2014)

The Wars of Napoleon
Charles J. Esdaile
(Longman, 1995)

Waterloo: Myth and Reality
Gareth Glover
(Pen & Sword, 2014)

WEBSITES

The International Napoleonic Society
www.napoleonicsociety.com

Musée de l'Armée
www.musee-armee.fr/accueil.html

The Napoleon Bonaparte Podcast
napoleonbonapartepodcast.com

The Napoleon Foundation
www.napoleon.org

The Napoleon Series
www.napoleon-series.org

The Napoleonic Association
www.napoleonicassociation.org

Le Souvenir Napoléonien
www.souvenirnapoleonien.org

NOTES ON CONTRIBUTORS

EDITOR

Charles J. Esdaile was educated at the University of Lancaster, and, after 15 years in the Department of History at the University of Liverpool, was appointed to a personal chair there in 2004. A specialist in Napoleonic Spain, his major publications include *The Spanish Army in the Peninsular War* (1998), *The Duke of Wellington and the Command of the Spanish Army, 1812-1814* (1990), *The Wars of Napoleon* (1995), *The French Wars* (1999), *The Peninsular War: a New History* (2002), *Fighting Napoleon: Guerrillas, Bandits and Adventurers in the Peninsular War, 1808-1814* (2004), *Napoleon's Wars: an International History, 1803-1815* (2007), *Peninsular Eyewitnesses: the Experience of War in Spain and Portugal, 1808-1814* (2008), *Outpost of Empire: the Napoleonic Occupation of Andalucía, 1810-1812* (2012), *Burgos in the Peninsular War: Occupation, Siege, Aftermath* (2014), *Women in the Peninsular War* (2014) and *Napoleon, France and Waterloo: the Eagle Rejected* (2016).

CONTRIBUTORS

Philip Dwyer is Professor of History and founding Director of the Centre for the History of Violence at the University of Newcastle, Australia. His primary research interest is eighteenth-century Europe with particular emphasis on the Napoleonic Empire. He is the co-editor (with Alan Forrest) of *Napoleon and his Empire* (2007), and the author of *Napoleon: The Path to Power* (2008) and *Citizen Emperor: Napoleon in Power* (2013). He is currently editing the four-volume *Cambridge World History of Violence* and the *Cambridge History of the Napoleonic Wars*.

Alan Forrest is Emeritus Professor of Modern History at the University of York. He has published widely on modern French history, especially on the French Revolution and Empire and on the history of war. His authored books include *Napoleon's Men: The Soldiers of the Revolution and Empire* (2002), *Paris, the Provinces, and the French Revolution* (2004), *The Legacy of the French Revolutionary Wars: The Nation-in-Arms in French Republican Memory* (2009), *Napoleon* (2011) and most recently *Waterloo* (2015), a study of the battle and its place in public memory. He has co-edited several works on the French Revolutionary and Napoleonic period, including *The Routledge Companion to the French Revolution in World History*, with Matthias Middell (2015) and *War, Demobilisation and Memory: The Legacy of War in the Era of Atlantic Revolutions*, with Karen Hagemann and Michael Rowe (2016).

Michael Leggiere is Professor of History at the University of North Texas. His research and scholarship focuses on the strategic, operational and coalition aspects of Napoleonic warfare. He has published five books between 2002 and 2015, two with the University of Oklahoma Press and three with Cambridge University Press. His first book, *Napoleon & Berlin: The Franco-Prussian War in North Germany, 1813* (2002) received the 2002 First Place Literary Award from the Société Napoléonienne Internationale. His 2014 monograph, *Blücher: Scourge of Napoleon* won the 2015 Society for Military History Distinguished Book Award for biography as well as the 2015 La Société Napoléonienne Internationale First Place Literary Award. In between, *The Fall of Napoleon, volume 1: The Allied Invasion of France, 1813–1814* (2007), won the 2008 Société Napoléonienne Internationale First Place Literary Award. All his books examine Napoleon's strategy and operations and the responses of his enemies between 1808 and 1815. Lastly, he was general editor of *Napoleon and the Operational Art of War* (2015).

Alexander Mikaberidze is the Sybil T. and Frederick Patten Professor of History at Louisiana State University-Shreveport. He has taught European history at Florida State

University and Mississippi State University and lectured on strategy and policy at the US Naval War College and US Military Academy. He is an award-winning author and editor of a dozen titles on the Napoleonic Wars, including a critically acclaimed trilogy on Napoleon's invasion of Russia. He is currently completing *The Napoleonic Wars: A Global History* for Oxford University Press and editing the *Cambridge History of the Napoleonic Wars*.

Frederick C. Schneid is Professor of History at High Point University in North Carolina, USA. He specializes in eighteenth- and nineteenth-century French and Italian military history. Among his numerous publications are, *European Armies of the French Revolution* (2015), *The French-Piedmontese Campaign of 1859*, (2014), *The Second War of Italian Unification, 1859–1861*, (2012), *The Napoleonic Wars* (2012), *Napoleon's Conquest of Europe: The War of the Third Coalition* (2005), *Napoleon's Italian Campaigns, 1805–1815* (2002) and *Soldiers of Napoleon's Kingdom of Italy* (1995). Professor Schneid also serves on the Board of Directors of the Consortium on the Revolutionary Era, and the editorial boards of the *Journal of Military History* (USA) and the *British Journal of Military History*.

INDEX

ACKNOWLEDGEMENTS

AUTHOR ACKNOWLEDGEMENTS

On a personal note, a brief word of thanks. In the first place: we have the editorial team who have guided me throughout the process, namely Sophie Collins, Caroline Earle and Stephanie Evans, all three of whom have been a joy to work with. And then there are my many fellow contributors, models of enthusiasm, co-operation, responsibility, patience and erudition one and all. To each and every one of you, thank you so much: it has been a blast (what else?)!

PICTURE CREDITS

The publisher would like to thank the following for permission to reproduce copyright material:

Archives départementales des Côtes-d'Armor: 147TR(BG).
Basque Digital Library: 117C(BG).
Biblioteca Museu Víctor Balaguer: 101TLC.
Biblioteca Virtual del Patrimonio Bibliográfico: 69CR(BG), 115TL(BG).
Biblioteca Virtual de Aragón: 101BL.
Bibliothèque nationale de France: 35CR, 35BR(BG), 35TL, 37CL, 37BR, 39TR, 39CL, 39BL, 39CL, 39TR(BG), 39T(BG), 43TL(BG), 45BR, 45CR, 45T(BG), 45C, 47BR, 47BR, 47TL(BG), 49CR(BG), 55TR(BG), 55BR, 57TR(BG), 57B, 63TR, 63BR, 65TL, 67B, 75B, 75TR, 77CR, 77CR(BG), 77TL, 87BR, 89TR, 89B(BG), 107TR, 107B, 115C, 115C(BG), 117BL, 117TR, 119BR, 121CR, 121BR, 125CL, 125TR, 125TL, 125BL, 127CR(BG), 129C, 129CL, 129TL, 129TR, 141CL, 141B, 141TR, 145BG, 145CFR, 149TR, 149TC, 149BL, 149BR, 149BC, 149CR, 151CR, 151CL.
British Library: 47CR, 83TL(BG), 83TR(BG), 89T(BG), 89CL(BG), 99T(BG), 109CR, 117TL, 119TR(BG), 121TR.
Clipart.com: 17CR, 17BR, 19TCR, 27TC, 39C, 43C, 49BG, 55TR, 89TL, 89B, 95B(BG), 101TR, 109TR, 122.
Fondo Documental Histórico de las Cortes de Aragón: 101BCL.
INP - National Heritage Institute, Bucharest: 125CR.
Leipzig University Library: 40, 60.
Library of Congress, Washington DC: 7, 23CL, 27B, 29T, 35TL, 37TR, 39BR, 43CL, 55C, 57TR, 79C, 83B, 87C, 138, 151TC.
Livrustkammaren, Sweden: 119R.
New York Public Library: 17TR, 35C, 77BR, 79TR, 129BR, 135T, 135BL, 135BCL, 135BCR, 135BR, 135BFR, 145CR, 149B.

National Gallery of Art, Washington: 77TR.
Österreichische Nationalbibliothek: 27TR, 43CR, 49CR, 49TR, 65TC, 67CR, 75TL, 79TL, 83TL, 85CR, 85CFL, 85CL, 87TR, 89TC, 117C, 119TC, 121C, 125CL, 127TR, 129C, 141TL, 143CL, 143C.
Rijksmuseum: 59BC(BG), 59R, 59TL, 59C, 109C.
Nick Rowland: 7.
Shutterstock/Alessandroo770: 17L; Andris Tkacenko: 19BR; Betacam-SP: 49CR(BG); Bildagentur Zoonar GmbH: 83C; DioGen: 149C; Dja65: 149C; DutchScenery: 151(BG); Emi Cristea: 77TC; ER_09: 17TC; Erofeenkov: 105TCL; Everett – Art: 2C, 23TL, 29C, 43BR, 45BL, 47C, 49B, 63C, 69TC, 85T, 97C, 97B, 105CB, 105TL, 109TL, 109B, 115B, 127C, 137TL, 137TR, 137C, 137BL, 137BR, 145T, 151BL, 151BC, 151BR; Fotosutra: 63BG; Galastudio: 99C; Georgios Kollidas: 19TL; Gino Santa Maria: 143B; Hein Nouwens: 25TR, 63TC, 63BC, 79CL, 89C, 127TL; I. Pilon: 2(BG), 47B(BG), 99BR, 135BG, 151BG; iBird: 37BL; Ivan Ponomarev: 17BC; Jag_cz: 115C; Jiri Hera: 19C; JirkaBursik: 99CR; k2photoprojects: 85BR; Kosmos111: 117BR; Laila Kazakevica: 2(BG), 135T(BG); Leonid Andronov: 95TL; Marzolino: 17BG, 29B, 49T(BG), 97C, 107C(BG); Michael Wick: 97CL; Morphart Creation: 19BG, 102, 121TL, 143CR, 85CR; Ntstudio: 83C(BG); Oliver Hoffmann: 107TC; Peace PhotoHunter: 15B; Photomaster: 19TCL; s74: 65TR; Scisetti Alfio: 19TR(BG); Sergej Razvodovskij: 145BR; Sergey Kohl: 43CR(BG); Shebeko: 83C(BG); Solodov Alexey: 79CR; Steven Wright: 55BL(BG); Tatiana Shepeleva: 99C; Tsuneomp: 23CR; VallaV: 29C, 37C(BG); Velora: 17BC, 115TL; Yamagiwa: 15C; Yurok: 55C(BG).
TopFoto/Roger-Viollet: 80.
VU University Amsterdam Library: 127BL.
Wellcome Library, London: 19TFR, 35CL, 47CL, 145CL.
Wikipedia/Jean-Pol Grandmont: 57TC; Jimmy44: 115TR, 117CL; JLPC: 147C; JoJan: 79B; Rama: 147T; Rauantiques: 37C; Sailko: 117CR; Sodacan: 55BC, 65CL; Tom Lemmens: 45C(BG); Tretinville: 121CR.
Yale University Art Gallery: 99BL.